BEFORE TRUTH
Set Me
FREE

BEFORE TRUTH
Set Me
FREE

A Fool's Journey from
Behind the Music to Behind Bars

Vanessa "Fluffy" Murray

DORAH PUBLISHING LLC

Dorah Publishing LLC
539 Atlantic Avenue #170155
Brooklyn, NY 11217
347.598.3321
http://www.dorahpublishing.com/

Copyright © 2021 by Vanessa "Fluffy" Murray

All rights reserved. No part of this publication may be reproduced, stored in a retrieval system, or transmitted, in any form or by any means, electronic, mechanical, photocopying, recording, or otherwise, without the prior written permission of the author.

This book is a memoir that read like a novel. All the events depicted are true and the characters are real. The events, conversations, and experiences detailed herein have been faithfully rendered as I have remembered them, to the best of my ability. Some names have been changed—three to be exact—in order to protect the privacy and/or anonymity of the individuals involved.

1st edition, © 2010

Cover design by Pamela of www.delaney-designs.com

Illustrations from the Rider-Waite Tarot Deck® reproduced by permission of U.S. Games Systems, Inc., Stamford, CT 06902 USA. Copyright ©1971 by U.S. Games Systems, Inc. Further reproduction prohibited. The Rider-Waite Tarot Deck® is a registered trademark of U.S. Games Systems, Inc.

Printed in the United States of America

ISBN-13: 978-1-7363583-2-0

TABLE OF CONTENTS

PREFACE .... **VII**

OPENING .... **XIII**

PART I **1**
IN THE BEGINNING

PART II **47**
BEHIND THE MUSIC

PART III **137**
SLEEPING WITH THE ENEMY

PART IV................................. **177**
STATE PROPERTY

CLOSING **247**

SNEAK PEEK............................ **253**
TWIN FLAME JOURNEY TO SELF-LOVE

PREFACE

Before truth set me free from the chains of psychological slavery, illogical religious dogmas, and flat-out lies designed to promote the white race as supreme, instead of love (the highest frequency in the universe), I believed just about every cock-and-bull story society fed me. I ate it all up as if it were good chicken soup for the soul, especially the greatest cock-and-bull story ever told.

You know the one: male Caucasoid—born by way of Holy Spirit and a virgin—is the Eternal Unbounded Source of Life, All-in-All, Supreme Being, Great Spirit, Big Banger of the Big Bang, Ineffable Energy Source, Infinite Intelligence, or—as many simply call It—God.

They told me I was a free will machine, but regardless of that I'd better accept this legendary Virgin Birth tale that's been passed down for generations—the same way racism's been handed down from generation to generation—or else there would be hell to pay: an eternal, super-duper hot barbecue pit created to roast not only wicked humans but also wicked lions and tigers and bears–oh, my!

Wait a minute! If I'm not mistaken, wasn't this burning hot pit called hell created to roast Santa Claus and the Three Fat Bears?

Whatever the case may be, I was shook! So, without logical evidence, without a critical analysis, without realizing I was actually being whitemailed, I wasted no time accepting this mythological, astronomical allegory at face value, especially when they broke it down like this: "Fluffy," they told me, "if it turns out the story is a lie, you ain't got nothing to lose. But girrrrrrrrrl, if you're a nonbeliever and it turns out to be true, I feel sorry for you, boo. You're doomed, finished, kaput!"

Well, since they put it like that, I went all out. I even hung a clock on my bedroom wall, an oil-painted timepiece of a bloody, nailed-to-a-stick, blue-eyed, long fair-haired, pale-pink Caucasoid.

Come to think of it, he looked like a hippie. I prayed to him. I worshipped him. And if you told me this hippie on a stick wasn't my knight in shining armor, who was one day going to come down from his invisible castle in the clouds and swoop me up to safety, I'd tell you the same things I heard my indoctrinators say: "You're the devil! You're going straight to hell when you die!"

And then I would shun you because, per my indoctrinators' instructions: "If there come any unto you and bring not this doctrine, receive 'em not into your house, neither bid 'em Godspeed. For he that bids 'em Godspeed is partaker of their evil deeds!"

My indoctrination, or programming, began immediately following my arrival on planet Earth. I came here decked out in a silky-smooth outer shell infused with heaps of carbon (most call it melanin), and I was one of the cutest little chocolate-coated goddesses on this planet.

However, the society of systematic white supremacy I was born into, with its white-superior-black-inferior propaganda, wasted no time persuading me that the color of my casing, texture of my hair, and size and shape of my nose were ugly.

And like all the other cock-and-bull stories they fed me, I ate this up, too…just like a good little-programmed robot who goes against her own inner spirit to accept the psychological conditioning of an anti-nature, global racist system of dominance created by genetically modified organisms (GMO) who classified themselves as white, a conditioning that was, in the beginning, whipped into her ancestors for an overlong period.

As a result—before truth set me free—I spent a significant part of my life feeling inferior, unworthy, powerless, confused, unloved, anxious, and fearful of everything: death, hellfire, success, and failure.

In essence, I kept my authentic-self (my God-Self, as I like to call it sometimes and at other times, my Higher-Self) caged in a self-imposed prison and allowed my fear-self (lower-self)—fashioned by society and archetypal forces—to sit in the driver's seat.

I let it drive me into the arms of angry, insecure, and abusive men who were also being driven by their lower-selves. I let it drive me out of a top-level seat in the music game. And if that weren't enough, I even let it drive me straight to the pokey—a maximum-security prison.

My daughter would be all right without me in the so-called free-world, I reasoned. She was 20 years old and a grandmama's girl (my mom). My son, on the other hand, had just turned 17 and was still a high schooler and a mama's boy. He was, in a sense, still attached to the umbilical cord.

Even though he was visiting my mom in New York City for the summer, he desperately needed and depended on the one who taught him how to drive a car, to provide for him, nurture him, and keep him on the right path. Without me around, he was sure to go astray—and astray he went.

It wasn't long before he quit his summer job at a New York A&P supermarket to join a local gang. It wasn't long before he started dealing crack. It wasn't long before he was sporting a stupid-looking, black teardrop, tattoo on his light-skinned baby face, next to the right side of his eye. It wasn't long before a knife was plunged into his lower back during a fight with rival gang members. It wasn't long before I was reading a story about my son in the *New York Post*:

"...shot during an apparent drug-related incident on an Inwood Street, police said yesterday...when an assailant opened fire on him at 10th Avenue and West 201st Street. The shooter fled...."

My son was taken to Harlem Hospital.

Now, as you embark on your own special journey to self-awareness, self-exploration, self-discovery, self-understanding, self-love, self-transformation, self-mastery... buckle up and brace yourself because your ride through this revamped and expanded edition is going to be one heck of a bumpy ride, a ride into a slice of my life BEFORE my Kundalini[1] (yes, I said it: koondə'leenee) and God-Self woke up and took control of the steering wheel—Before Truth Set This Fool Free.

---

[1] Kundalini: a Divine power or sexual-spiritual energy that lies dormant inside the human body. Once awakened, the Kundalini travels upward, zigzagging, super-fast, sort of like an electrical pinball or snake, hitting what many call Chakras; then BOOM! You fall into a delightfully-blissful semitrance, engulfed in this intense feeling of pure Divine Love; or at least that's my personal-spontaneous Kundalini awakening experience. Your experience may be slightly different if you've ever had one.

"To be free means to open your heart and your being to the fullness of who you are because only when you are resting in the place of unity can you truly honor and appreciate others and the incredible diversity of the Universe." — Ram Dass

OPENING

Three strikes—you're out! I tell myself as the sharp, cold metal of the handcuffs slide down my bony wrists and bite into my bloodstained hands as the arresting officer shoves me into the back seat of the police car that is taking me to jail for the third frickin' time.

With my hands cuffed behind me, I fall against the hard plastic of the back seat. My elbows are aching with the pressure of the awkward position; so, as I lean forward to try to find some comfort, I peer through the windows, all four—front, sides, and back—and see an ambulance pull up.

While the medics are strapping my antagonist in place on a gurney and hooking up an IV, I notice a bunch of nosey neighbors gawking at me as I play my role in this gory lifetime movie.

This must be a movie or a dream because this isn't how my life is supposed to be. I had it all mapped out and going to jail dressed in a brown form-fitting t-shirt, an ancient pair of rundown, dingy-white, New Balance sneakers, and some frumpy old gray lounging shorts—all spattered with blood—wasn't a stop on my map.

At this stage of my journey, I'm supposed to be rich and famous, draped in diamonds and pearls, just like the original Queen Bee (Lil Kim) who was once under the tutelage of my former colleague, Sean Combs.

No, I didn't stutter. You heard right. Puffy (P. Diddy, Puff Daddy, Brother Love, or whatever he calls himself these days) and I used to work together. The day I landed that gig at Uptown Records, I said to myself: you're about to blow uuuuuuuup! Within a few months' time, Puffy and I were promoted to top-level executives.

First, I was promoted from receptionist straight to the head of publicity: the department that arranges for feature stories, interviews, and record reviews in local and national newspapers, magazines, webzines, and all kinds of stuff like that.

Not long after, Puffy was promoted from intern directly to head of Artists & Repertoire (A&R): the department that locates and sign new talent.

"I think you're the youngest A&R in the music game," I said to Puffy. "I could have my friend, Sonia, write an article on you. She works at *Class Magazine*. Would you like that?"

In his new position and new office space adorned with music equipment—unlike mine, which was decorated with posters of Doug E. Fresh I'd cut out of *Word Up!* and *Right On!* magazines—19-year-old Puffy slid his scrawny legs off his desk and exploded straight up in his chair. A broad smile inched across his face.

"Yeeeeah! I wanna be in a magazine!" he replied. "Can you hook it up?"

"Okay. I'mma call Sonia and set up the interview."

As Puffy swiftly climbed the ladder to success, I whooshed down like greased lightning—ALLLLLLLL the way down to my current situation.

During the ride from where I am arrested on San Gabriel Avenue in Decatur, Georgia to the county jail on Memorial Drive, I maneuver out of the handcuffs and place my hands on my lap. When the police car stops at a red light, I contemplate escaping out of the side window that's cracked wide enough for my slender frame.

I envision placing the cuffs underneath the seat before sliding closer toward the window. The arresting officer isn't paying attention to me; she's looking down at her phone or something. I reckon this is the perfect time to make my move. Like a snake, I swiftly slither out of the window the same way I slithered out of those handcuffs. I fall on the ground—ouch! I'm okay—I think; I get up assuming a low partial squatting position, then I duckwalk 'round to the back of the police car. The officer is still unaware I'm now outside of the car. It's now or never, I say to myself; then, I make a dash for the nearest bushes.

Knowing that I wouldn't get far before being tackled to the ground and slapped with another charge, if I wasn't shot to death by a trigger-happy cop, I snap back to reality mad quick and remain seated.

Reluctantly, I slide the cuffs back on so that the arresting officer in the driver's seat doesn't suspect I just had the silliest of silly thoughts. I spend the rest of the ride thinking about where it all went wrong and the penalty I'm about to face for my idiotic actions...and the adverse effects of my time spent in prison on my two children—children who will now have both of their parents locked up and in different states, too.

We arrive at the county jail in less than ten minutes. The arresting officer turns me over to blue-eyed, middle-aged Detective Buice. The first thing he notices is my loose-fitting cuffs. So, he tightens them, then places me in the back seat of his unmarked vehicle. I try to take the cuffs off again, but this time, they're too tight. Oh well, at least he left my hands cuffed in front.

"Am I gonna get a lot of time?" I ask Buice.

"Yes."

"How much?"

"You're looking at...well now, let's see...the victim lost a lot of blood...you could be facing twenty years, but—"

Whatever else Buice says, I don't hear him; I'm too busy noticing that smirk on his colorless face. Does he think my going to jail is a joke? I'm not going to say anything else to him. It's apparent he's no fan of mine, which is understandable; nevertheless, those little smirks etched on his face, the ones I keep seeing in the rearview mirror, pisses me off.

He reminds me of one of those sleazy detectives I've seen in movies. You know the kind—a rogue detective like leading character Alonzo Harris in the movie *Training Day*.

We finally reach our destination. Buice exits the driver's side and walks on over to my side. He opens my door, and I step out of the car and onto the curb. I don't know where I am exactly, or what's about to go down; the only thing I know is that I'm in deep doo-doo.

We walk inside a big building, seems like some type of office building. Inside are employees, or maybe other detectives, sitting at their desks paying us no mind as Buice escorts me through the office.

We pass a bathroom. "Can I wash my hands, please?" I ask Buice.

We make an about-face, and I enter the tiny one-man bathroom first, with Buice close behind, still smirking. With the door wide open, he reaches over me and turns on the water, a little cold mixed with a little hot, then he continues to stand behind me while I stand in front of the sink.

Surprise he's allowing me to wash away some of the evidence, I catch a glimpse of myself in the mirror hanging above the sink. Whoa! Is that a crackhead staring back at me? I notice my afro is sprinkled with blood. It's only been a year since I first decided to embrace my natural hair.

In addition to the blood, there's dirt in my 'fro. Must've found its way there during the altercation that somehow had me sprawled out on an asphalt driveway, sprinkled with soil, and landed me in the care of Detective Buice. Now my once beautiful hair looks matted and stank.

I proceed to scrub my hands as hard as I can to remove the dried blood. Maybe it's just me, but this blood isn't coming off easily. Fragments of it are on the upper parts of my arms, too, but I can't reach way up there with these stupid cuffs on.

"Okay, let's go," Buice says after what seems like two seconds.

"I'm not finished," I mutter. "Can't you see I still have blood on my hands? Dang!"

"Excuse me, did you say something?"

"No, just talking to myself."

I imagine Buice couldn't care less about me getting cleaned up; after all, to some folk, I'm nothing but another black nigger. Maybe that's the reason he doesn't even bother to give me a paper towel to dry my wet hands. Oh well, whatever. I'll just let 'em drip dry.

We continue along; where we're heading, I have no clue. We stop in front of a closed door. Buice opens it and allows me to enter first. Even though I've never been in this room before, it looks familiar—just like one of those rooms I've seen on television, where those slime ball detectives throw the so-called bad guys so that they can give them the third degree or trick them into spilling the beans. The interrogation room! Yup, that's what it is!

I quickly scan the small, drab room and discover nothing in it but a small table, two chairs, and a slab of dirty carpet on the floor. The window, or two-way mirror, is pretty large, and I can't see a darn thing except for my reflection when I look in it. Even when I zero in on it, still nothing. I assume, just as on television, somebody's watching me from the other side.

Inside the lonely room, I guess Buice to be about six feet tall as he towers over my five-foot-two-inch pocket-sized frame. His light-colored hair, sprinkled with a dash of salt and pepper, is cropped short, and it appears his hairline is gradually receding.

If only he'd wipe that annoying smirk off his face for one cotton pickin' minute, he wouldn't be bad looking. The smirk makes him look devilish—speaking of the devil, is it fair to say the white man is the devil?

Oh, never mind me. That question used to pop in and out of my head—before truth set me free—mostly when I'd see photographs of smiling white faces encircling the dead black person they'd just lynched and castrated or live footages of white boys in blue gunning down (mostly) black people for no good reason at all, except for the fact that they're black, which, by the way, is a very good reason for a white supremacist or a devil—but, who am I to judge?

Buice seems fit, nonetheless. No beer belly protruding. He could actually be a ladies' man; not my type, though.

He tells me to stretch out my arms, and then he inserts a key in my handcuffs, the same key he used to tighten my cuffs, jabbing it in and out of the keyhole numerous times.

"I can't unlock the cuffs," he claims, still wearing that silly looking grin. "I'll have to get another key."

I don't believe him because as the saying goes: the devil is a liar.

He leaves me cuffed in the interrogation room for what feels like hours. In his absence, I lie on the stained, carpeted floor in the fetal position, shivering like a slave facing corporal punishment.

Feeling like the biggest loser in my grubby, blood-spattered clothes, I ruminate on how easily I'd allowed some random person to board my life train, causing me to spiral out of control, sliding off the rational track, straight into an emotional ditch. Why didn't I simply take the high road?

Dog-tired, I close my big brown eyes and plead my case to the Divine Energy Source I'm sourced from: forgive me, God, for all my wrongdoings; deliver me from evil; show me the true meaning of life. I'm tired, God. I'm tired of running on this treadmill, chasing after the wind. And God, while you're at it, please get me outta here! Pleeeeassseee!

Detective Buice's entry back into the interrogation room startles me.

"Can you please take off these cuffs?" I ask.

"I forgot to get the key," he says. "Have a seat."

I sit in a chair facing the entrance. He sits in the other chair, the one facing the two-way mirror, and begins grilling me. Since committing felonies isn't exactly my forte, I naïvely tell him snippets of my version of what happened. I even let him feed me details of what he believes happened as well.

"You started it, right?" he asks.

"No."

"You swung first, right?"

"Yes...I mean, no...I don't know."

"The victim didn't have a weapon, right? You were the only one with a weapon, right?"

"Yes...no...huh?"

Then I sign the confession statement he writes in pencil on a pad of lined paper, a statement that will probably be used as evidence to assist the prosecution.

As I continue to play my role as the protagonist—or an unseasoned perpetrator, according to my voluntary admission statement—I don't even realize I have the right to remain silent, even though I've heard it many times on television, and even though the arresting officer robotically recited that speech to me: "You have the right to remain silent. If you choose to give up your right to remain silent, anything you say can and will be used against you in a court of law..."

After Buice is through outwitting me, we return to his unmarked car, and he drives me around the corner to the booking facility, where he turns me over to a black female correctional officer.

Before he leaves, a key miraculously appears in his hand, and he unlocks my cuffs without difficulty—Things that make you go hmmm, as Arsenio Hall would say.

After I'm fingerprinted, photographed, and processed, the correctional officer ushers me to a small, ice-cold holding cell and hands me a plastic bag full of food, even though I have no appetite.

"Can I get a blanket, please?" I ask the officer. "I'm freezing in here."

"Don't have any," she says with a snap.

Inside the icebox are three other female detainees and by the looks of two of them, I assume they're crackheads; then again, they're probably thinking the same about me because, as the saying goes, when you point one finger, there are three fingers pointing back to you.

"Hey, girl. What's yo' name?" asks one of the crackheads.

"Vanessa."

"Vanessa, do you want yo' food?" asks the other crackhead.

"No."

"Can I have it?" they ask simultaneously.

I stretch out my hand. Both crackheads reach for my bag, and onto the dirty concrete floor goes all the contents: a cold bologna sandwich, a moldy orange, and a four-ounce container of milk that's spoiled, according to the date on the carton. They both scramble to pick up the nasty-looking food.

"I asked first," says crackhead number one.

"I did!" yells crackhead number two.

"Just look at 'em," whispers the third redbone detainee with the good nine-ether hair. "Dem crack ho bitches look like two starved scavengers."

After I spend several hours freezing my buns off, the officer opens the cell door and takes me to a nearby doorless cubicle. She hands me an oversized, wrinkled orange jumpsuit, then holds up a white sheet while I stand inside the booth and change out of my blood-spattered clothes into my jailhouse garbs.

I hand her my civilian clothes, and she throws them into a plastic bag; then once again, I'm placed in cuffs and escorted into an elevator by another female officer—a half-pint Latina.

"I heard choo be takin' off yo' handcuffs," she says to me in a Spanish-ghetto drawl. Standing several inches shorter than I, she looks to be in her mid to late 20s.

When I don't respond, she presses the number four button. As the elevator travels upward in slow motion, terror seeps through my body. I picture myself locked in a tiny cell with a big ol' burly stud-woman—yikes!

We finally arrive on the fourth floor, on the northeast side of the jail. There are six dorms—100 through 600—called pods. We stop in front of pod 300.

"Oooh, girrrl!" Miss Half-Pint says to me. "Choo going into cell 301 with that crazy girl. I feel sorry for choo."

A crazy girl? I feel a quiver of fear as thoughts of what may happen to me in a miniature cell with a loony-toon takes several spins around my mind. I mean, after all, I'm no real gangster. I'm not even a fake one. I see myself as nothing less than a dainty lady, despite my present condition. Besides, if you ask me, the real thugs and criminals are sitting in their high seat of honor exploiting the peasants they govern.

"Excuse me, señorita," I beg. "I don't wanna be in a cell with a crazy person. Can you please put me in another cell? Pleeeaaassse?"

"Nope! Choo no have no choice here, honey. Choo just does what'eber we tell choo. Besides, choo must be crazy, too. I heard what choo did."

The correctional officer sitting in the control booth pops open the metal door to pod 300. Inside, inmates are sitting around, all over the pod, wearing the same orange getup as myself; some, however, look like men, others scary, some are sitting in front of a colored television mounted on the wall, and some are in their cell either asleep or standing by their cell door observing the scenery, while others are sitting around at a table doling out cards for a game, I reckon of Spades. I feel all eyes trail me as Miss Half-Pint escorts me to my new home: cell 301.

PART I

IN THE BEGINNING

Rider-Waite Tarot Deck

"*The fool doth think he is wise, but the wise man knows himself to be a fool.*"

CHAPTER 1

At the start of my tour as an Earthly being, people who strongly believed in the supremacy of the white race were running amok, committing all types of cruel and barbaric acts, without the slightest compunction, against black people and those who sympathized with them, which is the reason Malcolm X, a human rights activist and prominent figure in the Nation of Islam, was in Los Angeles, California the same year I incarnated onto this planet.

Malcolm was out there in La-La Land delivering a stirring speech at the funeral service of Ronald Stokes, an upstanding black citizen, who was murdered by members of the LAPD. More likely than not, they were peace officers...I mean, race soldiers[2] who had joined the police department for the sole purpose of assassinating black people with impunity, which also explains the 2006 FBI report that states law enforcement departments had been infiltrated

---

[2] RACE SOLDIER is a term coined by Neely Fuller Jr (author of *The United Independent Compensatory Code/System/Concept*) that describes a white supremacist who obtains jobs in law enforcement solely to mistreat and/or murder citizens scot-free, mainly black citizens.

with white racists, extremists, Nazis, and Klansmen—but, I ain't one to gossip, so you ain't heard that from me. Blame it on the alcohol, or better yet, blame it on Jamie Foxx—same difference.

"Who taught you to hate yourself?" was the big question Malcolm posed to the black spectators at Stokes' funeral. "Who taught you to hate the texture of your hair? Who taught you to hate the color of your skin to such extent that you bleach it to get like the white man? Who taught you to hate the shape of your nose and the shape of your lips? Who taught you to hate yourself from the top of your head to the soles of your feet? Who taught you to hate your own kind? Who taught you to hate the race that you belong to, so much so that you don't want to be around each other? Noooooooo…before you come asking Mr. Muhammad does he teach hate, you should ask yourself: who taught you to hate being what God made you?"

Three months to the day later, Marilyn Monroe—a white American actress, model, singer, and major sex symbol—was found dead in her Los Angeles home from an overdose of barbiturates. Some say she committed suicide, others say she was murdered to prevent a scandal from toppling the presidency of John F. Kennedy.

The same day Marilyn died, Nelson Mandela—a South African anti-apartheid revolutionary who later served as President of South Africa—began serving twenty seven years in prison for inciting people to strike, for leaving

In the Beginning

the country without valid travel documents, and for spearheading the struggle against injustice.

Roughly three weeks later, Fannie Lou Hamer, a sharecropper who later became a spokesperson for the civil and human rights movement, attempted to register to vote, along with seventeen others. Of course, white supremacists weren't happy about that—duh—so they did what they do best: terrorized Hamer and the seventeen others.

Sick and tired of being sick and tired of white racists and all of their malicious tactics to keep black people disenfranchised, Hamer would spend the next umpteen years standing up against political racism even though it would cost her jail time and a vicious beating that would leave her with severe kidney damage, a blood clot behind one eye, and a permanent limp.

A couple months later, still in the same year I was born, Johnny Carson, a white American comedian, producer, actor, and musician, began his 30-year stint as host of *The Tonight Show*, while 12-year-old Little Stevie Wonder released his first record on Motown Records and James Meredith became the first so-called nigger allowed to attend the University of Mississippi.

Since the passing of the law to integrate schools, all hell was unleashed against any so-called nigger who attempted to test this law. Consequently, Meredith's admission was opposed by state officials and students, sparking a riot that left two dead, more than 25 marshals shot, and approximately 160 injured.

By the time I was brought forth into this low-vibrating, third-dimensional reality or hellhole (as some call it), to first learn polarity consciousness, and in due course, unity consciousness, a butt-load of bullshit was waiting to be dumped on me, too, *and I ain't even had breakfast yet.*[3]

---

[3] Phrase coined by popular YouTuber, Ralph Smart (Infinite Waters).

CHAPTER 2

During the season when plants bring forth leaves and flowers, Moms was chillin' at one of her sisters' apartment at the Manhattanville Housing Projects in New York City when she was hit with labor pains.

Her sister lived on the seventh floor, so she had to wait for the elevator, which seemed to take extra-long to scoop her up. But as soon as she reached the lobby of the building, she rushed outside, through the back way of the building, and flagged down a yellow taxi.

It was a little after rush hour on a Monday evening, but still, could Moms get to the hospital in time when her contractions were coming every two to five minutes?

"Take me to Metropolitan Hospital," she told the cabby. "Hurry! I'm about to have a baby!" Metropolitan Hospital was about a five-minute drive from the Broadway Hotel on West 101st Street in Manhattan—that's where Moms resided. Unfortunately, from her sister's place, it was going to be nearly an hour's drive. "My water broke!" Moms yelled out to the cabby. "Hurry!"

The cabby was barely midway to Metropolitan when my tiny head popped out of my 23-year-old mother's vortex; so, she told the cabby to make a quick detour to the nearest hospital. He swerved around and pulled up in front of Sydenham Hospital in West Harlem.

A nurse ran out of the hospital pushing a wheelchair and helped Moms out of the cab and onto the chair. We hadn't even made it inside the hospital when the rest of my five-pound body slid out; so technically, half of me was born in a taxicab, and the other half on the streets of Harlem the 21st of May in 1962.

Sydenham Hospital mainly served black and poor patients, many uninsured. Even though Moms worked as a teacher's aide at a nursery school on the upper west side in Manhattan, she still couldn't make ends meet. For that reason, she was on welfare, too, when I arrived, so Medicaid paid her hospital expenses.

Moms named me after the Academy Award-winning, white-British actress, Vanessa Redgrave. A few months after my birth, however, Moms started calling me Fluffy. Soon, everybody and their mommas called me Fluffy, too.

I was always fidgeting and shaking my legs and kicking around my crib blanket, a practice I still do today.

"That's why I nicknamed you Fluffy," Moms told me. "You were always fluffing the covers. Your legs never stayed still."

In the Beginning

I was my mother's middle child, and unlike most children, early on I was taught by one of my aunts to call my mother Millie instead of Mommy or something of that nature. I can't even picture children of mine calling me by my first, middle, last, or nickname, but I grew used to calling my mother Millie. In fact, calling her Mommy feels strange to me.

From the beginning of my earthly days, and long after, I was very quiet and remote. Millie swore to god I was an otherworldly being. She didn't understand, nor could she figure out, the divine air of mystery that surrounded me, and so, with well-intentions, she had my head examined by a couple of shrinks who could find nothing particularly wrong with me, except I didn't talk to them, either.

My distinctive personality—which, to me, seemed ordinary—irked Millie's nerves to such a great degree, I could not only feel her icy blast of disapproval, but I could see it written all over her face, especially when her upper lip would curl in disgust as she'd look down upon me and whisper to others: "She's weird," right in front of me as if being unique made me deaf, dumb, and blind, too.

So, early on, instead of learning how it felt to be loved, respected, and protected, I learned how it felt to be rejected and emotionally abused. I also learned early on, I was Millie's least favorite child—but, it wouldn't take a rocket scientist to figure that out.

My brother, Millie's firstborn (the golden child in her eyes only), came to be approximately one year before me. Millie named him after a white romantic, swashbuckling actor: Tyrone Power.

Ty was born at a so-called high-class hospital. It was considered high quality only because it catered mostly to those of European descent.

"Your brother was the only black baby in the hospital's nursery," Millie told me.

Ty was supposed to be born at Metropolitan, too, but Metropolitan was overcrowded on the day of his delivery; so, hospital officials placed Millie in an ambulance and drove her to the nearest hospital—Flower Hospital.

My first home was at the Broadway Hotel, of course. We lived there until Millie was in her second trimester with her next child. A tiny kitchenette in an aparthotel wasn't going to be big enough for Millie's growing family, so she moved us to a nearby, small one-bedroom apartment in a five-story walk-up tenement off Central Park West and 100th street.

By the time I was roughly 15 months old, Millie had given birth to her third and final child, my sister, Michelle, at Metropolitan Hospital—finally. I don't know who Millie named Shell after, but whoever she was, I bet your bottom dollar she was white and famous.

My siblings and I have different daddies. Of the three, we met one—my sister's dad, James. For many years,

In the Beginning

Millie told us James was the father to all three of us. But for some strange reason, he looked like none of us, except my sister, who was way lighter skinned than my brother and me. In fact, she looked like Janet Jackson.

My brother's coat of skin was dipped in a much darker chocolate mixture than all of us, and if I didn't know any better, I'd swear he played Kunta Kinte in the movie Roots, instead of LeVar Burton—yikes!

James didn't come around much, but when he did, he paid no attention to any of us little ones, and he contributed nothing financially, except once he gave me two pennies to add to my coin jar, which I still, till this day, continue to collect 'cause they come in handy every now and then.

His rare visits were mainly an attempt to have more sex with Millie. Although I was mad young, I still remember the last time he came to visit. It was 1960 something. It was late at night. My brother and sister were asleep on the bunk bed in the bedroom, and I was lying beside Millie on a king-sized bed in the living room.

Adjacent to the king-sized bed was an end table and a sofa. James was sitting on the sofa as his feet rested upon a beautiful area rug we later had to discard because one of my brother's badass friends puked on it and stunk up the whole apartment—pee-ew!

"Can you put her on the couch?" James asked Millie.

"No!" Millie yelled. "You sleep on the couch!"

From the sounds of it, she must've finally had enough of his romance without finance.

James sucked his rotten teeth, rolled his bloodshot eyes, muttered a few unkind words, and stumbled out the apartment with a fifth of vodka in hand.

After that day, we saw James a few more times, strolling the streets of Harlem, pushing a handcart full of frankfurters, and he'd always give us free franks. And didn't nothing taste better than a New York City frank in a bun, smothered with those famous New York City succulent onions. Mmm Mmm good!

All three dads shirked their responsibilities. My dad, perhaps, didn't even know I existed, or maybe he did. According to Millie, he sent his homeboy to the hospital to check me out when I was born.

"Your father," Millie told me, "looks just like you."

"I guess that means he looks like you, too," I said. Millie and I looked like twins. The only slight differences were our hips and buttocks—Millie had neither.

"Your dad's from Baltimore," Millie told me.

"What's his name?"

"James," she said. "James Shuler. He was on break from the Navy when I met him, and right before he went back to the base, he asked me to marry him."

"So why didn't you marry him?"

"Because I was confused. And I didn't even know I was pregnant when he asked. So, I told him, 'No' and he left and went back to the Navy. I never heard from him again."

Why Millie never tried locating my dad, so she could tell him the good news is still suspect. Wasn't I good news? Even when I tried prying info out of her, she never talked much about any of her baby's daddies, especially my brother's dad. The only thing she said about him was that she'd met him on the day he was released from prison. She's never even told us why he was in prison, or for how long.

Was he a rapist, drug dealer, stickup kid, or murderer? And, what was his name? She never told us that, either. I wonder if she even knows. Maybe his name was James, too.

CHAPTER 3

Our new apartment was on the third floor—apartment 3N. I'll never forget that place. Our windows faced a junkyard and a few times a year, robbers would climb up the fire escape leading to our windows, bend our cheap window bars, slip in while we weren't at home, and leave our apartment in a state of disarray after stealing everything of value to us, including my jar of pennies and Millie's record player.

A couple times they didn't know we were home and tried to break in, but our loud, fearful screams sent them screaming and flying off the fire escape to save themselves from us.

Furthermore, we had a big hole in the bathroom wall gnawed by rats; but, despite all of that, I loved our new home, it was the best I'd known at that point.

I'll never forget this one beady-eyed rodent that held Millie and me hostage in the bedroom. I'd just gotten through taking a bath and Millie was helping me put on my underclothes as I was recovering from the painful sting of spritzing my tight little yoni with perfume when suddenly, we heard a high-pitched squeal.

"What's that, Millie?"

"A mouse is caught in the mousetrap, Fluffy. C'mon, let's go see."

We tiptoed to the bathroom, which was connected to the bedroom, and saw this big, dusty-looking, beady-eyed rat—instead of a little mouse—squirming and squealing while trying to get his head from underneath the spring-loaded bar trap that had cheese placed on the trip to lure in our predators.

"Ahhhhhh! He's getting loose, Millie!" I cringed and jumped behind Millie, who was just as frightened as I was, though she tried not to show it.

"Ahhhhhhhhhh!" We both screamed as the rat wiggled his head from underneath the trap. He wasn't a happy camper, either. He appeared dazed. His nose was bleeding, and he kept flinging his head. Then the conniving little weasel charged us. We ran to the bunk bed and leaped onto the top bunk…breathless. We sat with our backs against the wall and waited; no sound. We leaned forward to peek down at the floor.

"Ahhhhhhhhhh!" That sneaky little rat bastard was right in front of the bed, staring up, mean mugging us with his black beady eyes. He snarled while looking at us from a ready-to-leap stance.

We slammed our backs against the wall again and waited—no sound. So once more, we slowly leaned forward to peer down. This time, he was ambling toward the bathroom, then suddenly he stopped and turned giving us one last angry look. If I didn't know any better, I'd swear I saw him roll his beady eyes before disappearing into the bathroom.

Millie and I hauled tail from the top bunk, closed the bedroom door behind us, and ran straight to the living room and onto the king-size bed where my brother and sister were sound asleep. We remained there for the rest of the evening.

Our community, now called Manhattan Valley, was a culturally diverse neighborhood that bordered Central Park. The mixture was one of the best things I loved about living there. Even the white people appeared to be sane and civilized compared to the ones wilding out all across the south, west, and Lord knows where else.

Growing up in an interracial environment gave me firsthand knowledge that not all individuals classified as white heartless or committed to the maintenance of white supremacy, even though, at the end of the day, most, if not all, enjoyed the extra trinkets that went along with simply being identified as white, and in some cases, being identified as an elite.

Unrelated to that, it wasn't unusual to find me and my sister hanging out on the fifth floor of our building at the apartment of one of our white neighbors who, by the way, we swore worked as a clown because of the massive amount of colorful makeup she wore.

Straight down the hall from us was a young, single Latino mother. She kept her front door wide opened (we did, too)—day and night—in hopes that her runaway child, Mona Lisa, who was my age, would someday return home.

It wasn't unusual when one of Millie's white co-workers paid us an occasional visit. Her name was Ann. She was the head teacher at the same nursery school Millie worked at.

Memories of her visits are still vivid. I looked forward to Ann's visits because she was not only warm and friendly—the same way I pictured those foreign colonizers must've been, at the outset, to the indigenous peoples in the Americas prior to wiping out many of them with disease, war, and slavery—but she also had long, thick, pretty, sandy-brown hair, too, and she didn't mind me playing in it.

I loved her hair so much so that each time she came by, I'd have her sit on the floor with her back against the sofa, then I'd grab a hairbrush, sit on the sofa right above her head, and spend nearly her whole visit brushing her beautiful long hair and wishing I had the same kind of hair, too—before truth set me free.

One of the other best things I loved about my neighborhood was Central Park, one of the best parks in New York City. We did everything there: bike riding, swimming, ice skating, roller-skating, and sleigh riding—so what if my siblings and I used cardboard boxes to slide across the snow?

My brother, Ty, was a natural-born daredevil. When the lake froze over in the winter, he'd walk on the ice. One day some thin ice collapsed, and just like that—he fell into the freezing water.

My sister and I didn't know what to do. We were like 6 and 7 years old—give or take. So, we stood at the edge of the lake and watched in horror as our dying brother frantically searched for the hole he'd fallen through. After several attempts, he found it and saved himself—whew!

The last thing I wanted to do was run home to tell Millie her beloved son was a goner and that my sister and I did absolutely nothing to save him the same way there was nothing I could do to save my son from drowning in the mean streets of New York City while I was locked behind bars.

Unfortunately, that near-fatal lake incident didn't stop my brother from taking risks. If he wasn't throwing rocks at our neighbors' windows, he'd pretend he was a stuntman or Spiderman and attempt all sorts of life-threatening exploits, including subway surfing on the I.R.T. train, nearly killing himself once again when he slipped and one of his legs got stuck between the platform and the moving train which dragged him about a hundred feet, almost onto the tracks before it made an emergency stop. This and many other antics gained Millie a headful of gray hair at an early age.

In the Beginning

Millie loved music, and she loved to sing. Not a day went by when she didn't have the radio or record player blaring soft rock or the sounds of Motown. She especially loved Gladys Knight.

Her earliest aspiration was to be a recording artist, like her father, Hallie Murray. "My father and his brothers recorded *Milky White Way*," she told me. I later learned that *Milky White Way* was afterward recorded by Elvis Presley.

My grandfather's singing career was short-lived because he decided that drinking alcohol was more important, even though his doctor warned him to stay away from the booze. His liver eventually gave out, and he died when I was still a toddler.

While I didn't know the meaning of death as a tot, I was happy to never see my grandfather again. I don't know why that was. All I remember was that every single time he came to visit us, I'd yell and scream and cry as if he was a monster or something yucky, especially when he'd pick me up. The last time he picked me up, I made sure to vomit all over him in hopes that he'd never pick me up again—it worked.

Unlike me, Millie could carry a tune. In the late 1950s, she and two other girls performed during Amateur Night at the Apollo Theater in Harlem. They escaped getting booed off stage, which meant they were good.

After their impressive performance, they found themselves a manager, who thought he made it clear when he told them, "As a rule, I don't like managing females because they always seem to ruin things by becoming pregnant. But there's always an exception to the rule."

21-year-old Millie and her group were on their way to the big time when she became pregnant with my brother; that was the end of her dream of being a famous recording artist. But that didn't stop her from singing Gladys Knight and the Pips songs all throughout our apartment.

Her love for music was so strong that she rarely missed a concert, especially Gladys Knight. I don't know how she was able to scrape up the extra funds for all the concerts she went to, but she did—and she took me and my siblings along with her.

I don't know about my brother and sister, but I loved all those concerts just as much as Millie. I loved watching James Brown, the sex machine, slide across the Apollo stage and dance like no one I'd ever seen. But the concert I remember most was the Jackson Five at Madison Square Garden, one of the biggest arenas in New York. I don't know how Millie pulled it off, but we had great seats, right up front near the stage. Come to think of it, we always had great seats, even at the Apollo.

I was around 9 or 10 years old and totally mesmerized by those fine young Jackson brothers singing their hit tunes, including *ABC, I Want You Back, The Love You Save, One More Chance,* and *I'll Be There*. When they sang their last song, they pulled a fast one on the audience. Those little jive turkeys hoodwinked us.

What happened was after they'd sung the last song they pretended they were going to sing another song. They got all geared up, music playing, as they stood in front of their mics, then whoosh! Without warning, they flew off that stage like a rocket, with all the young screaming groupies right behind them.

Even security couldn't tame those wild girls; they jumped onto the stage, bogarted their way past security, and chased the Jacksons backstage. I don't know how far those thirsty girls got, or if any of them caught their prey, but I understood why the Jacksons had to outfox their audience. Those girls were cray-cray for them boys—and so was I, but not crazy enough to chase them.

While at that concert, I fell madly in lust with Michael Jackson, who'd clearly stolen all of James Brown's dance moves. But my like for him wasn't quite as strong as it was for Diana Ross. In my eyes, no woman on earth was prettier and classier than Miss Ross.

Okay, there was one other beautiful looking woman: Snow White, who'd, like a caterpillar, transformed herself into a beautiful butterfly named Marie Osmond of the 1970s *Donnie and Marie Show*. But, my focus right then was Miss Ross.

For a long time, Miss Ross was all I wanted to be. I wanted to look like her, dress like her, and sing like her, even though I was tone deaf. Nothing else mattered. I went through that period desperately wanting to be this amazingly famous singer whose melodic voice—the one I didn't have—gave listeners goosebumps the way Diana Ross gave them to me.

I'd stand in front of a mirror with a hairbrush in my right hand, imagining it was my microphone. I'd wear a long black, silky straight, European, Cher-like wig that I'd begged Millie to buy me.

As I got older, I'd put on tight-fitting clothes and high-heel pumps and cake my face with too much make-up. You couldn't tell me I wasn't Miss Ross as I belted out, off-key, my favorite Diana Ross and the Supremes songs: *Stop in the Name of Love*, *Where Did Our Love Go? Love Child*, and much more.

I would later attempt to sing *Stop in the Name of Love* in a beauty pageant and was laughed off stage by a dumbass audience who didn't know the difference between a singer and a comedian, but that's a whole 'nother story.

After my looking-glass performances, I'd practiced my acceptance speech for all the Grammy, Billboard, and American Music Awards I'd surely win someday: I want to thank God for giving me my heart's desire. I want to thank all my wonderful fans, who love and support me. Last, but certainly not least, I want to give a shout out to all the men around the world who want me…call me!

CHAPTER 4

The year was 1978, the month of July. I'd just turned 16 and was working at my very first job as a summer youth assistant to the head counselor at a camp located in the Manhattanville Housing Projects.

I'd been smoking Newport cigarettes since the age of about 14. But one day while on break at work, I took a drag of my cigarette and it tasted horrible; then I threw up. Every day after, I'd vomit all day, and those nasty tasting Newports became a thing of the past.

Eventually, Millie suggested I take a pregnancy test and as she'd predicted, I was with child—approximately eight weeks pregnant during an era when teenage pregnancy was a pariah.

My first instinct was to get rid of it, but how? I was a minor who had no clue about matters such as this. This was grown folks' problems. So, I looked to Millie for the answer to my dilemma.

"Keep it," she said. "It sure would be nice to have a baby around here."

Even though that wasn't the answer I was expecting to hear, nor was I ready to be someone's momma and caretaker, mother knows best—as the saying goes.

As difficult as it was, I spent the rest of the summer working and throwing up until it was time to return to high school. By then, I was four months pregnant and showing. I was so embarrassed to be the only one my age, that I knew of, pregnant. So, I begged Millie to help me get rid of the baby growing inside of me before others would find out.

"Here," she said a couple days later, "take these."

I swallowed all the pills in the bottle, but nothing happened. I was still pregnant. I wondered what went wrong; why didn't a whole bottle of drugs make the baby disappear like she said they would?

Evidently, the placebo effect backfired on me but worked precisely the way Millie had hoped. Those fakeass, dummy pills didn't even make me sick.

"We think it would be best if you went to a school for pregnant girls," officials at Louis D. Brandeis High School told me. "Once you have the baby, you can return to Brandeis."

The school for pregnant girls was in an East Harlem brownstone. There were less than twenty pregnant girls at the school, and we were all forced to leave our mainstream schools because school officials believed it was shameful for a teen to walk around an ordinary high school knocked up.

In the Beginning

I was in the tenth grade when I should've been in the eleventh grade. Unfortunately, Brandeis held me back the previous year because I'd played hooky nearly every day. Brandeis sucked! None of my homegirls from junior high school were students there, and I made no new friends to goof-off with, so, I saw no real need to waste any more of my precious time and energy attending another public school just to continue to be primed and trained on how to memorize a bunch of stuff and nonsense such as black people evolved from monkeys.

"No!" I blurted out to a white male teacher teaching that malarkey to a classroom of all black students. "We do not come from monkeys!"

Why didn't he teach us about the Rh Factor, the Rhesus Monkey Blood Factor as it is called? Why didn't he teach us about the consequences such as miscarriages, rhesus hemolytic disease, or death to the mother that can occur when, let's say, an Rh-negative woman carries an Rh-positive baby? Why didn't he teach us stuff like that, important stuff?

I never wanted to attend Brandeis in the first place. I wanted to go to Norman Thomas High School, where students at least learned shorthand and typing, but I wasn't accepted there because my grades weren't up to par. I'd played hooky in junior high school, too; so much so that a truant officer paid me a visit once or twice.

My baby's father (baby daddy) was a low-rolling drug dealer I'd met the winter of 1977 while he was posted up on a Washington Heights' street corner doing what drug dealers do. He was 17 years old and unbeknownst to me, a few days prior to meeting me, he'd just been released from Phoenix House, a drug rehab in the Bronx where he'd been living for the past two years.

As for me, I'd recently been dumped by my second boyfriend. My first boyfriend is someone I met when I was 14. He deserted me like this: "We've been together for three weeks," he said. "if you don't have sex with me, I'm going to quit you because I'm not going to be in a relationship with someone for a long time and not have sex. So, what's it going to be? Are you going to have sex with me or not?"

"Nope!" I told him.

"Then it's over!"

"Okay. Bye."

My second boyfriend (may his beautiful soul rest in peace) dumped me when one of my so-called best friends went to his home and told him I was having sex with multiple boys behind his back, even though, at this point and time of my life, I was still a virgin—a 15-year-old virgin and the new kid in baby daddy's town.

That's right! My Mother had moved us miles away from Central Park West, but Washington Heights wasn't the first new neighborhood we'd moved to, it was the second.

In the Beginning

The first one was a neighborhood located directly across the street from my junior high school and Manhattanville Housing Projects (where my aunt and some of my first cousins resided). I'd just turned 11 and moving from Central Park West to 129th Street and Amsterdam Avenue was one of the worst days of my life.

I begged Millie to at least allow me to continue to attend P.S. 163 (Alfred E. Smith elementary school) on west 97th Street and Columbus Avenue. I'd finally broken out of my non-talking spell and made friends in school. I even had a best friend. Her name was Deidra. She was the new girl in my fourth-grade class. My teacher sat her right next to me, and before the end of her first day, she and I were inseparable.

"Please, Millie," I begged and begged and pleaded. "I don't want to go to a new school. Can't I just take the bus to 163 every day?"

"No," Millie said. "I'm putting you in P.S. 161." That was Pedro Albizu Campos School.

As you can probably imagine, oppose to Alfred E Smith (a multiracial school with predominately white teachers), Pedro Albizu Campos was predominately Hispanic, and as you can also visualize, I went right back into my no-talking cocoon. But worse than that, I cried every day for my first best friend.

The apartment on 129th Street was another five-story walk-up tenement. In fact, the building was down the hill from Convent Avenue, a neighborhood coined Da Hill, perhaps because you had to walk up a steep hill to get to Convent Avenue.

It's the same community multi-platinum selling hip-hop artist and Grammy Award winner Kool Moe Dee raps about in one of his classic songs, *Wild, Wild West*: "*I used to live downtown, 129th street, Convent, everything's upbeat, parties, ball in the park, nothing but girls after dark, we chill, nobody gets ill, in the place we call Da Hill...*"

The inside of the apartment was made like a train and all the cars...I mean rooms...were connected in a line. Before long, Millie was having a mutually beneficial relationship with one of the tenants. He was not only a tenant, but he was also the building's superintendent, and he was white—a wrinkly-old white man named Wally.

Like most people around the globe who've been manipulated and had their brains whitewashed by the social engineers of the world and one of their most powerful brainwashing machines (mass media), Millie was not exempt from having her mind controlled, too.

So, after having had several bad experiences with black men, Millie decided it was time to take a dip in the white pond. She'd finally adopted the same attitude as a lot of programmed black people, like Mariah Carey's ex-husband, Nick Cannon, who, unfortunately, believes dating or marrying a white person is an upgrade or symbol of success—I beg to differ, though.

I loved hanging out at Wally's apartment because a talking, colorful parrot lived there, too.

"Polly want a cracker?" I'd ask the parrot.

"Polly want a cracker? Polly want a cracker? Polly want a cracker?" it mimicked.

It wasn't long before Wally became like family. So, when we moved to Washington Heights, he sort of moved in, too. I mean, he had a key and he was there all the time. He'd even sleep over two or three nights a week and, financially he was a big help, even buying us our very first 19-inch colored television.

No longer did we have to use pliers to change channels on our 13-inch black and white TV until, a few weeks later, my brother, the golden child, stole our new 19-inch to support his crack addiction, and, once again, we were back to using pliers to change channels on our 13-inch.

Although Wally wasn't the only white man in the picture, he outlasted the others and would remain a part of our family for over a decade. Then one day I noticed he hadn't been to the house for weeks.

"What happened to Wally?" I asked Millie.

"Oh. He died," she told me in a nonchalant manner.

"How?"

"AIDS."

"How did he catch AIDS?"

"He caught it from sharing needles and having sex with that dope fiend he left me for."

The news was shocking and disturbing to me because Wally had become the only father figure I'd ever known. He was in my life from the time I was 11 until my 20s. Why we didn't attend his funeral, if he even had one, still puzzles me; but he will never be forgotten, at least, not by me.

The Washington Heights neighborhood was by far the worst neighborhood where we'd ever lived. It was always noisy and heavily plagued with poverty and crime. The streets were swarming with drug dealers, addicts, and number runners. And it seemed like nearly every morning, news of another soul from the neighborhood had been found shot or stabbed to death.

Our apartment was another five-story rat-ridden walk up. The mice in our apartment were intolerable. They were everywhere—a whole colony of them. They even crawled in bed with me. One of them even had the galls to crawl underneath my covers and nibble on my big toe. After that night, I rarely got any sleep because I had to stay awake to shoo those yucky creatures away from my bed.

Ben took the cake, though. I was home alone one day. Thirsty, I headed toward the kitchen and stopped dead in my tracks at the entranceway when I spotted him moseying toward the stove.

At first glance, I thought I saw a black cat. How did it get in here? It must've wormed its way inside via an opened window, I thought. But when I saw his tail—long and hairless—I knew that the animal before me was no frickin' cat.

Ohmygod! It was a frickin' Ratzilla! A Nutria or an affiliate of the Gambian giant pouch rat family. He was humongous. I'd never seen a rat that size until then, and as I quietly tiptoed out the front door, I prayed I never would again.

CHAPTER 5

February 3, 1979

At the age of 16, I gave natural birth to a beautiful five-pound girl at Columbia Presbyterian, a hospital four blocks away from our Washington Heights apartment. It was the same hospital that had pronounced civil rights leader, Malcolm X, dead on arrival.

Baby daddy, now 19 years old, tried to comfort me in the delivery room, but he was no help. He screamed like a frightened little girl and blurted out, "Ugggh!" as he nearly fainted at the sight of all the blood and guck that flowed out of my pearly gate and booty hole. So, doctors escorted him right on out of the delivery room until he regained his composure.

He was so excited to be a father for the first time, even though he really wanted a boy. "My baby ain't gonna want for nothing," he told me while puffing on a cigar. Although he wasn't a cigar smoker, to my knowledge, he claimed smoking cigars was customary after a baby was born.

I wondered if yelling out of a window at the top of your lungs, numerous times, "I'm a daddy!" was a tradition, too? 'Cause that's what he did while smoking on that cigar with a couple of his buddies.

A few days after giving birth, I went back to Columbia Presbyterian to get myself on birth control pills. I told myself I was not going to get knocked up again. No, siree! The pain of giving birth was too excruciating. Ohmygod! It was the worst kind of pain I'd ever felt…that is until years later, August 25, 2012 to be exact. That was the year a lot of twin flames' heart chakra was opened and activated when Kundalini did its transformation there, at least mine was.

So, what's so painful about that experience, I bet you're wondering? Nothing. It was the events that followed that caused an indescribable agonizing pain to my soul—the labor pain of spiritual rebirth and no more contact with my twin flame, which was divinely orchestrated. But, all of that is a whole 'nother story for another book—speaking of another book, I've inserted at the end of this excursion an exclusive sneak peek of a page from the upcoming sequel to this book.

After I picked up my birth control pills, I went back to the teen pregnancy school to finish out the remainder of the tenth grade because there I could bring my newborn. I figured it would be in my best interest to return to Brandeis after the summer break, when my daughter was a little older. However, after summer recess, I had a change of heart, and I didn't go back to Louis D. Brandeis, except to tell school officials, "I'm dropping out!"

Millie tagged along to support my decision to become a high school dropout and to make sure school officials didn't try to talk me out of it.

In a strange kind of way, consciously or subconsciously, she wanted me to follow in her footsteps, to teach me a lesson about sneering at some of the choices she made to make ends meet, or at least that's the message I got when she told me, "Now you're gonna have to sleep with men to provide for your child."

By the time my daughter was five months old, I was pregnant again. Those birth control pills and I didn't quite click; I hated popping them every day, so I didn't. But I didn't want to have another baby, either, especially while juggling an infant at the tender age of 17. So, I thought it best to get an abortion this time.

If I'd known then what I know now: abortion is just another form of murder, I'd never have done it…perhaps.

After I ended my pregnancy, I obtained a free babysitter through some type of voucher program for low-income families, and then I found employment as a cashier at McDonald's on 34th Street, downtown Manhattan. I hated that job, and it obviously showed.

"You're fired!" my supervisor told me after I'd worked there for two whole months.

"Why?"

In the Beginning

"I don't like your attitude, that's why."

But for a few quick seconds, I was hardly sad about losing that job. I thought an office job would be a better fit for me, at least until I was rich and famous. But how in the world was I supposed to work in somebody's office if I couldn't type even ten words a minute? On top of that, I didn't have a high school diploma. But, it didn't take me long to figure out my next move.

After I earned my GED, I copped a job as a bank teller at the Union Dime Savings Bank in Spanish Harlem. Baby daddy's grandmother babysat this time. She lived right across the street from me in the Washington Heights neighborhood. The arrangement she and I worked out was great until one day I didn't show up on time to pick up my daughter.

Baby daddy was pissed, to say the least, so instead of helping me out this one time by picking up our daughter until I arrived, he left her in the care of his grandmother and paced up and down the hood, awaiting my return.

As soon as he saw me, he quickly approached me and punched me in the stomach, while I was carrying his third child, unbeknownst to the both of us that day.

Then he snatched my hoop earrings out of my ears before kicking me in the stomach; then he grabbed me by my jacket's collar as he commenced to drag me down the street. I somehow managed to break free from his grip and flagged down a police car that happened to be riding by in the nick of time.

As I was telling the two young black officers baby daddy was beating the crap out of me, baby daddy interceded and calmly explained to them that I was his girlfriend and that we were simply having a little disagreement about nothing.

For some reason the officers didn't seem to believe I was in dire straits—maybe because baby daddy didn't punch me in the face this time, so my face was intact—and as they were about to pull off, leaving me all alone with my abuser, I cried out to them, "Please don't leave me here with him! He's gonna beat me up worse than before."

"Do you want a ride, Miss?" they asked.

"Yeah." I quickly jumped in the back seat and told them to drive me to Manhattanville Housing Projects before bursting into tears. And, due to my predicament, I didn't get a chance to pick up my daughter at all that day so that was the last time baby daddy's grandmother babysat our child.

I was still a teen—nineteen—and pregnant for the third time. I was quickly heading down the same path as my mother, walking in similar shoes.

I felt trapped in a loveless, passionless relationship. The only minor difference between Me and Millie was that she was at least over 21 years old before she had her first child.

So as before, I quickly made plans to have another abortion. I didn't want to be like my mother. And telling baby daddy I was pregnant again, and on my way to abort the child he'd kicked and punched, seemed pointless, so I didn't tell him.

By this time, I was fed up with being his punching and kickboxing bags. Besides that, he didn't help at all nor did he keep his end of the bargain when he told me, "My baby ain't gonna want for nothing."

The few times he'd given me money, he'd turned right around in the wee hours, swearing, kicking, and banging on my door, demanding it back. Millie usually convinced me to give it back to him because he threatened to beat me up if I didn't.

If it wasn't for Craig's help (one of his best friends), some days I wouldn't have had any money to feed and diaper our child. (May Craig's beautiful soul rest in peace.)

Young and gullible, I had no clue that demanding money in the wee hours was one of the signs exhibited by crackheads. How was I supposed to know baby daddy had relapsed when he always wore clean clothes and fresh new kicks?

And how was I supposed to know he was a stickup kid, too, when he never took me with him on his robbery sprees nor did he discuss that part of his life with me?

It wasn't long before his lifestyle landed him in prison, and that's where he'd ended up spending the greater part of his life.

I was all ready and set to have abortion number two. Millie tagged along and sat in the waiting room while I was escorted into the procedure room. I laid flat on my back, legs propped up, moments away from terminating another pregnancy, when suddenly a boyish-looking Caucasian nurse walked in.

She wasn't the same nurse who'd stepped out of the room moments before and told me she'd be right back to perform the abortion. Nope. She was a different nurse.

"Vanessa," she said. "We're not going to give you an abortion."

"What?" I shrieked as I sat up. "Why not?"

"I'm sorry. We can't do it here."

"Why not? I don't want to have this baby."

"Would you like to speak with a therapist?"

"For what? I just want an abortion!"

Moments later I found myself in another room, smaller than a jail cell, sitting across from another Caucasian-looking woman with long black hair, wearing a white lab coat. No way was this her office, I thought. It was way too tiny. Inside was a small table with two chairs and no therapist couch. If I didn't know any better, I'd swear we were sitting inside of what used to be a mop closet.

"Why are you crying?" the therapist asked.

"I want an abortion, and the nurse won't give me one. Do you know why?"

I can't remember the entire conversation, but I remember it was as empty as the look on her colorless face. The therapist acted as eerie as the nurse, and just as the nurse, she

In the Beginning

gave no explanation to my simple question. I stormed out of her office, weeping like a baby, and into the waiting room where Millie sat, tears streaming down her face, too.

"Why are you crying?" I asked Millie.

"I don't want you to get an abortion," she confessed for the first time. "Why are you crying?" she asked me.

"I want an abortion, and they won't give me one."

Millie's face lit up as she jumped and clapped for joy.

"I don't know why you're so happy. I'm gonna go somewhere else to get it done. I don't want another baby!"

I tried to make sense of that bizarre day. Why was I given no explanation whatsoever? I tried to make sense of Millie's behavior, too. Why was she so concerned about the life of my third fetus when she didn't care that I'd aborted my second one?

I tried to make sense of the fact that I never did make an appointment at another abortion clinic. And, when I became pregnant for the fourth time (five years later by another man) after giving birth to my third fetus, of course, why was I then successful at aborting my fourth fetus, too?

Who was this third fetus that I couldn't abort (or lawfully murder) as I had abominably done to my second and fourth fetuses? And the nurse that refused to give me an abortion...was she really a nurse or an angel in disguise?

June 27, 1982

I gave birth to a five-pound, two-ounce, beautiful baby. Baby daddy wasn't there for the delivery of his second born; as a matter of fact, baby daddy and I hadn't spoken to each other for nearly six months prior to the birth of this mysterious child.

As far as he was concerned, he wasn't this child's father because a couple months before knowing I was pregnant, I had confided in baby daddy that someone had tried to rape me. The attempted rapist demanded I not scream, but I did anyway, as loud as I could, and he got scared just as I'd hoped and so he didn't complete the task. Afterward, baby daddy went on to tell others, including members of his family, that I'd been raped and therefore, the baby I was carrying wasn't his.

So, even when baby daddy and I'd see each other in the streets, we'd walk past each other as if we'd never met. And I could tell by the look on his face that if I'd even said, "Hi," he'd have probably punched me in my face. He, and some of the people he told, made me feel like it was all my fault that some man had tried to rape me. And I would forever regret telling him.

But the day baby daddy heard through the grapevine (my moms, I'm sure) that I'd given birth to a light-skinned baby boy who looked exactly like him, and nothing like the dark-skinned attempted rapist, he rushed to the hospital where I was moments away from naming his son, Kevin Murray.

"Vanessa, please name him after me," he begged and pleaded, as tears rolled down his face. "Please, baby! Please give him my name!"

CHAPTER 6

Three months after the birth of my son, whom I'd named after baby daddy, Millie quit her 9-to-5 as a waitress at Chock full o' Nuts Coffee Shop and took over as my permanent in-home babysitter.

By this time, she had long since resigned from her job as a teacher's aide, even though she'd been offered a position as head teacher if she'd pass the GED test. She wasn't interested in either, is what she told me.

No longer a bank teller, I'd enrolled in Katharine Gibbs, a predominately white private business school located midtown east.

"You're going to school? Millie asked. "Don't you think you need to get a job instead? You need money, not an education."

"I can't get a good job if I don't go to school to learn a skill."

"I didn't plan on babysitting just for you to go to school. I thought you was gonna get a job?"

"I am…after I graduate. The school is only for one year."

In the Beginning

In 1983, I earned a certificate in word processing from Katie Gibbs. Because the school catered to mainly white people during the early 80s, it had a good reputation; it was known as one of the best secretarial business schools in New York City, the elite of New York's business schools.

Now that I was typing over 60 words a minute and proficient in the Wang and IBM Displaywriter (microcomputers), the school's employment department offered me an opportunity to work as a typist in a typing pool at the White House in Washington, DC during the time President Ronald Reagan was serving his two terms.

I desperately wanted to take that job, but as a single, 21-year-old parent with two small children (1 and 4), I had no clue how I was supposed to wing it in DC. Who would babysit while I went to work?

I politely declined the offer and settled for a job in a typing pool, in the legal department at the Division of Housing and Community Renewal (DHCR) as an information specialist, a fancy name for word processing operator or typist.

During this time, my craving for spiritual food kicked in. I wanted to know things like: How was this magnificent universe created? Why am I here? What's my purpose? Why is there so much hatred and violence in this world and little love?

I sought answers to my many questions by watching all types of religious television programs, such as Jimmy

Swaggart and Reverend Ike; I read lots of Jehovah's Witnesses books and magazines that Millie had laying around the house.

I spent hours upon hours reading the Bible without understanding that most of the stories in it are allegories and not to be taken literally; and several times a week I went to church—various ones—looking for God, not realizing...God is within you (Higher-Self)...and, so is the devil (lower-self).

At the age of 22, I got baptized at a Baptist church in Harlem. It wasn't the last time I got baptized, but it was my first. 'They' told me I had to do it—get immersed in water—if I wanted to avoid roasting for an eternity in that barbecue pit called hell.

After my baptism, I talked about nothing but sweet Jesus—the name commonly used in Christianity, the name I called on before truth set me free.

"You know, you really shouldn't spend so much time in church, talking about Jesus. You're too young for that. You should get out and experience life and date lots of men and have fun," one of my aunts told me.

I took into consideration my aunt's advice, and before long, I was craving the entertainment world as much as the spiritual world. I was drinking out of two cisterns, but truthfully, the entertainment world had the spiritual world beat by a mile or two.

It wasn't long before I took an unnecessary three-month leave of absence (and never returned) from my decent and secure, though a tad boring, state job as an information specialist to work temp assignments—dumb.

It wasn't long before I stopped going to church and placed the book about the Sun—I mean, the Bible—back on its shelf to collect dust as I set out to chase after fame, fortune, and along the way, a big-time rap star.

PART II

BEHIND THE MUSIC

Rider-Waite Tarot Deck

As above, so below

CHAPTER 7

In my dreams, he was my boo, but in reality, he was nothing more than a pathway to a gig I'd never even considered.

The first time I saw him in person was at the Silver Shadow nightclub, where he was scheduled to perform. It was 1985. I'd managed to worm my way right up to the front of the stage; I had to get close up on my boo, who was sporting a head full of curly curls. Thank goodness there wasn't any greasy activator juice dripping from his curls—yuck!

For three nights in a row, after his dazzling performance at the Shadow, he was all up in my dreams. The dream that stayed in my head the longest was the one where I stood in a silent desert, wearing a long, white flowing gown. He crept up behind me and twirled me around to face him. His touch startled me, but he quickly calmed me down, gently grabbing my face with his two big hands. He slipped his wet tongue in my ear, kissed my neck and then *wham*! He thrust his tongue in my mouth; seconds later he had me moaning and groaning as he tongued me down for what seemed like an hour. After the long, passionate kiss, he undressed me, threw my gown across the desert, and we made wild, crazy love in the sand. We did every position imaginable—doggy style, missionary, cowgirl, standing, sitting, T-square, sixty-nine, wheelbarrow—until the break of dawn. I was in seventh heaven. On the verge of exploding into an orgasm, I woke up drenched in sweat, disappointed that it was only a cotton pickin' dream.

He was one of the biggest rap stars of the 80s. He had a unique way of using his mouth to imitate drum machines and samples of oldie-but-goodie tunes, and he became known by many as the Original Human Beat Box and the Greatest Entertainer.

I was totally in lust with homeboy, and I had to find a way to turn my dreams into reality. I just had to meet him but how? I couldn't be just another groupie, or at least I couldn't let him know I was precisely that. I had to be much more if I wanted to get his attention. I needed a master plan, so I put on my magician's cloak and thinking cap to devise a grand scheme to capture my boo.

I made up my mind to search out jobs that would allow me to meet and mingle with celebrities. I convinced myself that as an industry insider, I was certain to bump into my boo.

I didn't know it then, but it's been said, and or written, that when you want something bad enough, all of the universe will conspire in helping you to achieve it.

So, full of zeal, I submitted my resume to entertainment firms, and it wasn't long before I received a phone call from Gloria, the managing editor of *Black Teen Magazine*.

"I received your resume, Vanessa," Gloria said. "Unfortunately, we don't have any openings here at *Black Teen*. What I would like to offer you is a position with another publication we're in the process of starting up. It's called *What's Hot*, but it'll be a few months before that publication is up and running."

"Sounds marvelous! I would love to be a part of *What's Hot*," I told her.

My conversation with Gloria was fairly brief, but during our pleasant exchange, I casually asked her why my boo hadn't ever been in any issues of *Black Teen Magazine*.

"I've been trying to get an interview with Doug E. Fresh for quite some time," Gloria replied. "I can't seem to get one."

That was all I needed to hear. "I can get an interview with Doug E. Fresh!" I blurted out.

"Oh, really? And how are you going to do that, Vanessa? If I can't get an interview with him, and I'm the managing editor, how are you going to get one?"

"I can! I just know I can! He's performing at the Red Parrot tomorrow night, and I plan to be there. I'll let you know how the interview turns out."

"I highly doubt you'll get an interview, Vanessa. As I said, I've been trying to get those folks at Reality Records to set something up, but they never do. I've placed Doug E. Fresh and his management on my shit list."

After we hung up, I danced the wop all around my bedroom, shouting, "Yes, yes, y'all! To the beat, y'all! I'm in the house, y'all! God is good, y'all!"

CHAPTER 8

My plan to meet Fresh was in full swing. The Red Parrot was a huge, trendy nightclub in Manhattan between 11th and 12th Avenues on 57th Street where big-name artists such as Madonna performed.

A neon parrot, ten or eleven feet high, stood in the entrance hall. Real live red tropical parrots lounged the night away in soundproof glass cages; when partygoers tapped on the glass, the birds couldn't hear anything outside that glass, it seemed.

There were three bars. The main bar, closest to the dance floor, had five to seven bartenders working at the same time. The passageway leading to the dance floor was fenced in with chrome wire.

I frequently patronized the Parrot, so I knew my way all around that joint. What's more, I'd had the pleasure of performing live on the Parrot's rotating see-through glass stage months before Fresh's performance.

I was one of three backup so-called models for Milk and Gizmo, a local rap group collectively known as the Audio

Two. Most hip-hop heads knew them for their hit single *Top Billin*, off their 1990 *What More Can I Say* album.

The Audio Two and their manager-dad spotted me and the other two models, Purple and Peggy, at a beauty pageant rehearsal held at a downtown Manhattan club.

Milk and Giz had a few shows lined up and were at the pageant rehearsal scouting out a couple of cute girls to prance around them on stages around town to help promote their first 12-inch single, *A Christmas Rhyme*.

Their dad noticed Purple and Peggy and instantly recruited them. Purple, 20 years old then, was a striking Puerto Rican with long, black silky hair. She resembled the recording artist Vanity or some even said she looked like Halle Berry.

Peggy, a sensual, dark-skinned sister who sported a long, lustrous weave, later went on to become a video vixen, as well as a background singer for Diana Ross. She was about 21 years old, then.

Nat Robinson, the Audio Two's manager-dad, was especially smitten with Peggy. He was so busy drooling over her, he didn't even notice me, a 23-year-old who could pass for 17. Fortunately for me, 18-year-old Giz noticed me.

Although the gig at the Parrot was our second or third performance with Audio Two, it was the first big show, a show with major artists on the bill, and Purple, Peggy, and I would be on the same bill, performing to a packed house. I was mad hyped!

I wore the same outfit I always wore—a leopard dress clinging to the contours of my petite, shapely body. There was a split up one of the sides and the dress fell right below my knees. Purple and Peggy wore formfitting outfits, too.

Scheduled to perform that night were the female group 9.9, famous for their 1985 hit *All of Me for All of You*. There was also Val Young, famous for looking like a black Marilyn Monroe, and for her 1985 album, *Seduction*, which was produced by Rick James. To top it all off, Rick James showed up to support her.

"Can I take a picture with you?" I asked Rick as he and an older woman sat on the staircase leading to the dressing rooms.

"No," he said. "I'm trying to spend time with my mother right now."

Oh, please! Spare me the baloney! I thought, rolling my eyes as I walked away. Fifteen minutes later, I spotted him taking a picture with Peggy. Oh, snap! Not only did he take a picture with her, but he also seemed to drool all over her the same way Nat Robinson did.

Later that night, Peggy told me that not only Rick but also comedian Eddie Murphy had tried to get the hook-up and had given her their phone numbers. Guess I didn't have the right look.

Also scheduled to perform that night were rap stars Salt-N-Pepa. They were promoting their first single, *The

Show Stoppa, a response or dis track to Doug E. Fresh's hit single *The Show*.

As is normal in the music biz, we arrived at the Parrot a few hours before showtime for sound check. Salt-N-Pepa showed up, too. They weren't there long before a big, black grisly-looking man went ham on them.

"Get out of here!" Grisly Man yelled.

"Come on, Sandy," Salt said while walking toward the exit. "Let's just go."

"Nah, this shit ain't right," Pepa said, nearly in tears, while trying to stand her ground. "He can't do us like this. Fuck that!"

Pepa refused to leave and continued to yell back at the big, beefy man. A puny dude I'd invited to be my guest claimed he knew Pepa personally, so he walked over to her.

"You need some help?" he asked.

"Nah, I'm all right," Pepa said.

"Get the fuck out of here!" yelled the grisly man again, walking fast toward Pepa.

I was scared for her. Grisly Man looked as if he was literally going to pick her up and throw her out of the club.

"This shit ain't right!" Pepa yelled and cried as she reluctantly stormed out of the club in a fit of rage moments before Grisly Man could reach her.

Showtime!

The Audio Two were the opening act, and Purple, Peggy, and I joined them on stage. We had no routine rehearsed, so the three of us sashayed around Giz and Milk as if we were high fashion models.

"They ain't nobody," I overheard a couple of haters in the audience yell out as they watched us strut our stuff.

"Coming to the stage next is Super Nature!" the emcee announced.

Loud cheering erupted from the audience but then lo and behold, two scared-looking tackheads pretending to be Salt-N-Pepa (aka Super Nature) stepped on stage right behind the microphones. Of course, I wasn't surprised to see a fake Salt-N-Pepa, not after witnessing the way Grisly Man handled the real Salt-N-Pepa during sound check.

The cheering instantly stopped. "Who the hell are they?" partygoers demanded to know.

When the fake Salt-N-Pepa opened their mouths to lip sync *The Show Stoppa*, all I heard was "Boooooo! Get your raggedy asses off the stage! Boooooooooooooooo!" And I ain't ashamed to admit I was one of the booers.

After all, the real Salt-N-Pepa were my favorite female rappers, and there was no way I was going to stand there and let those two tackheads—bless their young hearts—pretend to be Sandra Denton and Cheryl James. No, siree! Those two young girls didn't stand a chance at replacing the real Salt-N-Pepa.

What Grisly Man failed to comprehend was that Cheryl and Sandy had generated a lot of fans from that one song in a short period of time, and it was much too late to replace them because everybody knew what they looked like. At least every young hip-hop head in New York City did.

The night Doug E. Fresh was scheduled to perform, I arrived at the Parrot extra early to beat the crowd. It was mid-spring or summertime, 1986. I was aware security didn't get beefed up until the place was nearly packed—usually around midnight—giving me fewer bouncers to sham while I tried to sneak to the dressing rooms to find my boo.

I usually went to the Parrot with Purple, sometimes with my other homegirl, Butter. This night was special. It was business, not pleasure. And I didn't want any distractions, so I went alone. Besides, it was harder to slink around with others tagging behind me.

Wearing a semi-conservative two-piece beige pants outfit, I stood near the entranceway leading to the stairs to the dressing rooms, while preparing a bogus story to tell the on-duty bouncer, who blocked the stairwell. Lucky for me, I didn't have to sham up anything because the bouncer suddenly left his post. I dashed up the stairs, and as I neared the top flight, I heard lots of people talking and laughing. One of the dressing rooms' doors was wide open. Some of the guests were in the room, while others stood outside the room, in front of the doorway.

"Excuse me," I said, pushing my way through the crowd. I scanned the small room and found him. He stood in the middle of the room, surrounded by his guests. He was tall, dark, slender, and mouthwatering. As I strode toward him, he saw me coming and looked me dead in the eyes. My heart skipped a beat, but I managed to remain calm. I stopped right in front of him, eye to eye. He ignored everyone else and continued staring me down. I could tell he was curious to know who I was and what I wanted. I had his undivided attention as I extended my hand to shake his.

"Hi, Doug E. Fresh. My name's Vanessa. I'm a reporter for *Black Teen Magazine*. Can I interview you?"

"Sure," he said without hesitation. "Let me introduce you to my road manager, and he'll set it up."

He escorted me a few steps across the room to an elderly Latino man whose hair was sprinkled with a lot of salt-and-pepper. Fresh introduced us and instructed his roadie to set up the interview, then Fresh shook my hand once again and left me standing with his roadie as he went back to finish entertaining his guests.

The road manager gave me a time and place to interview Fresh. I thanked him and like a magician who had just executed a successful magic trick, I quickly disappeared out of the dressing room, bursting with excitement.

CHAPTER 9

"I have a doctor's appointment this afternoon," I lied to my supervisor. "Can I take the rest of the day off?"

"No, you can't!" he yelled. "If you leave, don't come back!"

It wasn't a difficult choice. Was a measly temp assignment more important than interviewing Mr. Fresh? This was, perhaps, my only chance to shoot my shot, and I was going to let nothing or nobody stop me. I grabbed my purse and jacket and said goodbye to one of my co-workers.

"Vanessa, you're going to lose your job over Doug E. Fresh?" my co-worker asked, giving me the 'you're-so-stupid' look.

"I can always get another temp job, but I can't always get the chance to interview Doug E. Fresh," I said as I walked out.

I stopped at an electronics store to purchase a sixty-dollar cassette recorder, then rushed over to a warehouse in Hell's Kitchen, a neighborhood on the west side of Manhattan, to see my boo.

When I arrived at the indoor video shoot, I rang the doorbell. The roadie opened the door and instead of a welcoming smile, I got a frown and a lame excuse that was intended to convince me to leave.

"You'll have to wait until the shoot is over before you can interview him. That could be hours."

"I don't mind waiting," I said.

A tad annoyed that I didn't go away, the roadie escorted me to a game room. Inside, I met Fresh's little brother and a few of his friends.

"Who are you?" they asked.

"I'm a reporter for *Black Teen Magazine*," I told them as I whipped out my tape recorder. "And who are you?" I asked a young dude lining up balls on a pool table.

"I'm Doug's best friend."

"Is that so? Why don't you come have a seat over here and tell me all about your relationship with Doug E. Fresh."

He was only too happy to oblige, and so was Fresh's younger teen brother, whom I interviewed later. I spent the next couple hours hanging out in the game room, enjoying the company of Fresh's friends and his brother until one of the video girls came into the room.

She told me her name was Shana and that she was 17 years old. She told me her mother was Susan L. Taylor, the former driving force behind *Essence Magazine*. I could see the resemblance.

Shana was wearing a short, black, tight-fitting skirt, with a yellow top the length of a mini dress, covering the top half of the skirt. She had a big black belt around her waist, and most of her hair was pushed back into a long ponytail, except for a wide bang that reached her eyelashes. She was very cute, just like her mother.

She gave me a look that appeared to say, *I'm hating on you,* then she questioned me about who I was, how old I was, and why was I there. Initially, I didn't like sista girl's attitude, and I wondered if she was dating Fresh. After some time passed, though, I realized she was a sweetie pie who was hardly hating on me; that was just a figment of my imagination.

I was having such a great time that I decided to share some of it with my friends. I called my two Puerto Rican homegirls, Purple and Ester, and told them to come on down to the shoot.

"Bring a camera with you, Ester," I said before hanging up the phone.

When they arrived, we all hugged and kissed, then headed straight to a room where Fresh and his crew were shooting their video for *All the Way to Heaven,* one of Fresh's songs off *Oh, My God,* his first album. They were lip-syncing and dancing on a stage shaped like a phonograph record. Ester immediately started snapping away like a professional photographer.

During one scene, Fresh wore a couple of big gold chains around his neck, white sweatpants, and a red wife beater with the word "Bally" on the front. Fresh, his crew, and the teeny-bopping video girls swung their heads from side to side, their arms moving in the same direction. I couldn't take my eyes off Fresh. He saw me watching him and waved. I wanted to pass out; instead, I smiled and waved back.

The shoot finally ended around ten o'clock that night. Fresh and his crew and me and my crew all entered a stairwell that would lead us back to the game room, one flight up. I heard Fresh's voice right behind me, so I turned around to reintroduce myself only to find him looking at my gluteus maximus.

Inside the game room, Fresh and I sat face-to-face on a sofa. He was sweaty, but he sho 'nuff looked good to me. I hoped I looked good to him in my black leather-looking four-inch slides, white ankle-length tight cotton skirt covered with black polka dots that accented my curves, and a black sleeveless mock neck that showed off my toned arms.

While my crew and his crew played pool, I whipped out my cassette player.

"Do you mind if I record you?"

"No, I don't mind."

I pressed record and took out a white five-by-eight pad with a list of questions I'd prepared the night before.

If Fresh sees me with a recorder and a list of questions, he'll no doubt believe I'm the real thing. Isn't that how real reporters do it? I thought.

"Why are you reading your questions?" Fresh asked. "I like reporters that speak straight from the heart."

He was probably unimpressed with my goofy cassette player, too. I should've bought one of those cute little hand-held voice recorders, but the goofy player was less expensive. Oh, well.

Slightly embarrassed by his comment, I ignored his request to put away the list and continued interviewing him.

"So, what type of kid were you?"

"Noisy. I used to stand on the tables in the lunchroom, rapping over beats that another kid made banging on the food trays. Some days, me and Barry B and Chill Will cut school and hung out at Barry's house, playing music and practicing raps and eating peanut butter and jelly sandwiches."

"How did you get into the music game?"

"At a New Edition concert. The crowd was getting restless waiting for New Edition to perform, so I got on stage and rocked. I had the crowd going wild."

Since my main quest was to become acquainted with Fresh on a personal level, I needed to find out if he was boo'd up and whether we were compatible.

"Is there a special lady in your life?" I asked.

Fresh paused for a split second, showing me a sheepish grin. "The only special lady in my life right now is my mother. I don't have time for a girlfriend right now because I'm on a mission with no luggage. After I finish the mission, then whoever I find that can deal with me, I'll be with that person."

Delighted to hear that my boo didn't have a significant other, I continued.

"What qualities do you look for in a girl?"

"Sweet personality, and very nice. She must understand me and what I'm doing. At the same time, if she respects me, then I'll respect her in return. I also want someone who wants to have a lot of children because I like children."

Fresh interrupted our interview to crack a few jokes on his little brother, who was nearby playing Pac-Man. As the brothers went back and forth joning each other, I chuckled at their silly jokes.

Before Fresh turned his attention back to me, he yelled out one last crack, "You dirt rag!"

I laughed out loud, and before long Fresh roared with laughter, too.

The interview continued, but this time the 19-year-old Fresh hurled a few questions at me.

"How old are you?"

"Twenty-four."

"You don't look it. Who did you say you work for?"

"*Black Teen Magazine.*"

He was silent for a moment, as if in thought while gazing longingly into my eyes. Then, with a knowing smile, he spoke. "You're clever."

I was cold busted. He knew I was really a groupie pretending to be a reporter. I mean...technically, I hadn't been hired yet, but was hoping I would be. So, I turned my attention back to my pad and hit him with the next question.

"Your latest single, *Nuthin*, is a rap against crack. How do you feel about the drug problem in our society?"

"Crack is simply the devil in another form. Leave crack alone!"

"How do you want people to perceive you?"

"I try to write rap songs that have a message because I don't want people to perceive me as being a street kid with no dollars and no sense."

Fresh's roadie walked up and interrupted us. "The owner is ready to lock up. Vanessa, if you want, you can finish the interview while we're walking out."

I decided to end the interview on the sofa with one last question.

"What are your future goals?"

"To put out the biggest rap record in history, win a Grammy, attend law school, and buy my mother a house in Barbados."

I thanked Fresh for his time as we stood up, then he gave me a hug and kissed me on my cheek. I wanted to scream, Hallelujah! But, as a new member of the press, I had to remain poised and professional; the groupie scream came out later when Fresh and his crew were far out of sight.

CHAPTER 10

I couldn't wait to tell Gloria how easy it was for me to cop an interview with the Original Human Beat Boxer. Oooh, I couldn't wait! I called her the next day.

"Whaaaaaat?" she shrieked when I told her how it all went down. Gloria was heated. "I can't believe this! I'm going to let Doug E. Fresh and his managers have a piece of my mind. I cannot believe they let you interview him, and not me. Oh, hell no! You're not even a real reporter."

"Now I am," I mumbled to myself. After Gloria finished venting, I told her I'd taped the whole interview. "I'll make a copy and send it to you in the mail."

I took it upon myself to write a story about Fresh, too. It only made sense to me. After all, I was the one who'd orchestrated and conducted the interview, so why should someone else write the story?

When Gloria received my package, she called me to say she was very impressed and that she was going to publish the story I wrote in the next issue of *Black Teen*. I was elated.

"Did you take any pictures, Vanessa?" Gloria asked.

"My friend, Ester, took a whole bunch of pictures, but none of them came out right, so no, I don't have any pictures."

"That's okay. I have a picture of Doug E. Fresh. I'll use that."

Before long, *Black Teen* hit the newsstand. Gloria sent me a big glossy tear sheet of my story, a copy of the magazine, and a check for fifty bucks. I was overjoyed for days, even though Gloria botched my story by adding something she had no business adding. Because of that, I had to explain the reason for the false addition to Fresh when I later ran into him at a celebrity party I'd crashed.

"I didn't tell you I was a Jehovah Witness," Fresh said.

"I know. Your best friend said that. The editor listened to the tape of the interview. She thought you said it, so she took it upon herself to add it to my story without my knowledge. I'm sorry."

Even with the mix-up, I was grateful to Gloria for publishing my first piece of writing. I'm the real thing now, I told myself—a professional writer.

I couldn't believe what I had manifested: my very own story with my very own byline was actually in a magazine that thousands of teenagers read each month, and at the bottom were the words: *Vanessa Murray is a freelance writer based in New York City. This is her first story for Black Teen.*

It felt good to see my story and byline in a magazine. It made me feel like some sort of big cheese, and I wanted to keep feeling like that. My lust for Fresh didn't make me feel like that; in fact, chasing after him made me feel more like a thot; so, my craving for him abruptly took a back seat to writing.

When Gloria didn't call me soon enough for a job at *What's Hot Magazine*, I certainly wasn't going to sit around and wait. I was more than ready to conjure up some more magic. For starters, I was eager to see my byline in print again, so I whipped up my resume, inserted my new accomplishment, and submitted it, along with my Doug E. Fresh clipping, to other publications.

It wasn't long before I received a call from Rene John Sandy, Publisher of *Class Magazine* and a huge admirer of Marcus Garvey. Voila! He offered me a position right over the phone, sight unseen.

He hired me to be the assistant to the editor; however, my job entailed assisting no one. I worked solely on my own as a reporter and writer for the publication. I made appearances at luncheons, parties, and various social gatherings. Sometimes I'd walk up to public figures and interview them right on the spot, but most times their publicists arranged the interviews.

One publicist didn't appreciate me interviewing his client without his permission. He rolled up on me and his client, actor Carl Payne (Cole, of the Martin Lawrence sitcom), one evening while we sat at a two-man table at a New York City nightclub.

"What's going on here?" the publicist demanded.

"She's interviewing me," Carl replied.

"For what? Who are you?" he asked me. "I didn't set this up."

I told Carl's angry publicist my name and the name of the magazine I was working for and handed him my cheesy business card.

"Before you publish a story on my client, I need to see it first!" he demanded.

I didn't appreciate his snotty attitude, so I ignored him and his request and turned my attention back to Carl as the angry publicist disappeared into the crowd—poof.

"Showtime!" someone announced over a loudspeaker.

Carl and I pushed back our chairs and rose, then quickly made our way to the front of the stage. We wanted no problems seeing Bobby Brown perform songs from his 1986 debut album, *King of Stage*.

Life at *Class* was short-lived. As it turned out, the company had financial issues; as a result, I rarely got paid. Eventually, a few employees, as well as myself, had enough of Mr. Sandy's excuses nearly every payday, so we all called it quits.

Not only was I out of a job, but I was also without a place to live. After living in the Washington Heights community for a decade, that jig was finally up, too. Around the time I'd seen Ben in the kitchen, we'd received a notice to pay up or vacate the premises. Our rent hadn't been paid for several months—at least six months. In fact, it hadn't been paid ever since Wally stopped coming around.

Although losing your home isn't cute, I was hardly upset about moving out of that nasty rat-infested building. No human should have to share their apartment with a gang of rodents.

So, me and my two children, my sister and her children, and my mother moved in with my aunt and her children at Manhattanville Housing Projects. My brother couldn't join us because as usual, he was incarcerated somewhere upstate New York with baby daddy.

After several weeks of living at my aunt's place, she and one of her daughters told me to get out, if I didn't give them money toward their extremely high phone bill, which wouldn't have been outrageous every month had it not been for a whole bunch of collect calls from my cousin's incarcerated baby daddy.

Meanwhile, I didn't have a steady income, so I couldn't contribute the large amount they demanded I pay, even if I wanted to. Plus, no one charged them one red penny when months prior they moved in with us into our two-bedroom Washington Heights apartment because their first apartment in Manhattanville Housing Projects caught fire and burned to a crisp. So, for about five months, they lived with us rent free, phone free, and food free until their new four-bedroom apartment, in the same Projects, different building, was available. They obviously forgot about that, or did they? And my aunt, likewise, forgot about the numerous times she used to ask me for money, and I never turned her down.

The truth of the matter is, the phone bill was really a bogus justification for the cruel treatment I underwent, something that had started long before this occasion. By this stage of my life, Millie had done an excellent job of pitting her sister and most of my family members against me to have allies, which now reminds me of the day she sat my then toddler daughter on her lap and told her to call me a witch. I winced, aghast at my mother's cruelty, as my daughter looked at me and repeated those words, not even understanding she was being conditioned to be another accomplice.

Sadly, the rejection and emotional abuse that began when I was a child didn't stop when I became an adult. It got worse—before truth set me free.

So, after I packed a shopping cart with some of my belongings, I was kicked to the curb on a sunny summer day, late in the afternoon, to begin living my life as a bag lady.

Right, wrong, or indifferent, it didn't make sense to me at that time to have my children roam around homeless, too, so I left them at my aunt's place, in Millie's care.

I spent the next several weeks pushing my raggedy cart from one friend's house to the next, and whenever I'd sleep over at my then best friend, Christina Rodriguez's apartment, I'd usually get my children and have them sleep over with me since they were living in the same community.

I also went back to temping, here and there, until the day I came across a tiny ad in a local newspaper: *Receptionist wanted at an entertainment firm.*

CHAPTER 11

The ad didn't include the name of the entertainment firm; so, I had no clue who or what was seeking a receptionist; and frankly, I really didn't give a hoot. I just wanted a job in anything pertaining to entertainment.

So, I submitted my resume to an address on Warren Street and 4th Avenue in downtown Brooklyn, and a few days later—during a moment in time when I was living at the Salvation Army on the east side in downtown Manhattan—I received a call to my room from Sandra Zuniga, the company's office manager. "Can you come in for an interview?" she asked.

About a week after the interview, in the autumn of 1988, I was the receptionist at Uptown Records, a relatively new management firm whose roster included recording artists Heavy D, Al B. Sure!, Guy, Groove B Chill, Finesse & Synquis, Father MC, The Gyrlz, and Mary J. Blige (who signed in 1989).

Right around the time I joined the Uptown staff, the CEO, Andre Harrell, had recently received a large sum of money to merge with MCA Records, located in Manhattan on West 57th Street, in the same building and on the same floor as Motown Records.

It wasn't long before half of the Uptown staff moved to Manhattan to share office space with MCA, but before that day arrived, and before I, too, would move to the Manhattan office, my new job as the receptionist of Uptown Records was stationed at the same address where I'd submitted my resume.

It was at a two-story condo owned by Andre Harrell. The living room, on the main level, was my domain. A kitchen, small bedroom (that had been turned into an office), and a small bathroom were on that level, too. Down the spiral stairs were three small bedrooms turned into offices and occupied by other employees, including Andre Harrell and his pretty assistant, Jill Woodlon.

As the front desk receptionist, I got to meet and greet a lot of wannabe and real celebrities who'd pop up often, including Aaron Hall, a member of the double platinum selling R&B group called Guy. Since Aaron lived in one of the units in the same condominium, he'd stop by the office quite often. Sometimes he came alone, and other times he came with big vicious looking dogs.

"Nuh-uh," I'd say. "Don't bring them in here."

Comic Chris Rock popped up sometimes, too. He'd usually sit in the reception area cracking jokes until he left. He kept me rolling in laughter as if I was at one of his comedy shows, except I was the only member in the audience.

Although my short-lived writing career had shoved Doug E. Fresh to the back of the bus, I was still very much a fan and always happy and excited to see him when he'd stop by the office.

During one visit, I invited Fresh into the upstairs bedroom...I mean, the small office, to show him all the posters of him I'd pinned on the wall.

Big Daddy Kane, another favorite rapper of mine, stopped by, too. The first time he came by, I could tell he was surprised to see me there when he looked at me wide-eyed as if he'd just seen a ghost. He usually saw me on Wednesdays at Harlem's famous Apollo Theater for Amateur Night, vying with other young ladies for his attention.

Like Doug E. Fresh, he, too, was at the top of the rap game in the 80s, so I was bowled over when one day, months before my tenancy as the receptionist for Uptown, he gave me his phone numbers—like three or four different numbers, including his grandmother's number. When I called him three weeks later, he was shocked, too.

"I can't believe you took this long to call me!" he said.

"Why?" I asked.

"Girls usually call me right away," he said.

When Kane invited me out to dinner one day (prior to Uptown), I didn't hesitate to go because I always felt a good vibe around him; he was mad cool and down-to-earth. In fact, he made me feel like I was the celebrity instead of him.

We met up at the Apollo, and it wasn't long before a bunch of screaming honeybees came out of the woodwork to swarm around my date.

"Pull me away," Kane whispered to me. "Pull me away from them."

I did not want those thirsty bees to sting me for snatching away their sexy, hot chocolate, so I let him figure out on his own how to worm himself away from them.

After he broke free, we hopped into his rental, but, before he drove me to Junior's Restaurant in downtown Brooklyn, where rapper Just-Ice and his date was oh-so-conveniently sitting within talking distance to us, he handed me some tissue and said, "Wipe that shit off!"

I took the tissue and commenced wiping off the pile of foundation packed on my silky-smooth face. This wasn't the first time he'd demanded I remove my makeup and told me I didn't need it and how much he hated to see pretty women wearing mounds of makeup.

As we were driving down the highway, he thought it would be a good idea to step on the gas. The car went over 100 mph, and while I was screaming and yelling at the top of my lungs, "Slow down, Antonio!" Kane was dying laughing like a homicidal maniac. He reminded me of Anthony Perkins who played a crazed, jealous photographer named Sean in the 1975 movie Mahogany, starring Diana Ross as Tracy, the most successful model in the world.

Except for that terrifying long scary moment on the FDR Drive, Kane behaved like a picture-perfect gentleman throughout the whole night, even though, in hindsight, he had the ideal opportunity to sexually assault me when we stopped at his residence after dinner.

Toward the end of the night, when we left his apartment and landed in the lobby near the entrance, he did attempt to kiss me—to no avail—before we exited the building.

In the end, he never once touched me inappropriately or asked me for sex, before driving me safely to my doorstep.

Dick, one of my favorite co-workers, spent a lot of time hanging out in the reception area with me because he didn't have an office and because he enjoyed my company. I could never figure out what his job entailed. I didn't even know his job title if he even had one; all I knew was that he kept me amused except for the time he stood in the kitchen, straight across from my desk, to show me what he was working with.

"Look, Vanessa," he said.

"Oooooh! I'm telling Andre on you!" I shrieked, turning my eyes away.

"No, Vanessa, please don't tell Andre," he pleaded as he quickly tucked his big black ding-a-ling back into his pants.

"I'm telling, you pervert!"

"Vanessa, noooooo! Please don't tell. I'm sorry. Please, please, don't tell Andre."

"Okay. But you better not do that again—pervert!"

Except for that offensive occurrence, Dick was a nice guy. I'll never forget the time he took up for me. He'd invited me to hang out with him after work, no place in particular.

"I need to make a stop at Carl's house," Dick said.

"Okay," I said.

Carl, a New York City cop by day and security guard for some of Uptown's events by night, lived a couple blocks from the office, so Dick and I walked over after work. After Carl invited us in, I made my way to a sofa in the living room while Dick stood near the front door, conversing with Carl.

Moments later, Carl's roommate, another New York cop, arrived home. When he saw me sitting on the sofa, he came and sat beside me. Then, with a big uncanny Kool-Aid grin on his face, he leaned down toward the floor and began grabbing my shoes as if he was trying to remove them from my feet.

"What are you doing?" I asked.

He didn't respond. He just kept grinning while struggling to take off my shoes. I tried to push him away, but he didn't budge and continued to wrestle with me. "Stop!" I finally yelled.

He paid me no mind. It made no sense to me. Dick, still communicating with Carl on the other side of the room, heard my cry and saw what was going down.

"Stop it, man!" Dick demanded. "She's not like that!"

At that moment, I realized what this cop was trying to do to me. But why the shoes first? Did he want to see if I had bunions on my toes or dirty, crusty heels like one of those reality stars of Love & Hip Hop, before sexually assaulting me?

"Come on, Vanessa, let's go," Dick said.

I was happy to comply. As we walked to the nearest corner to flag down a cab, we made no mention of what had almost transpired between me and that shady cop.

CHAPTER 12

Winter 1988

I heard a knock at the front door and opened it. Several teenagers with country accents barged in. I noticed two of them were exceptionally good-looking, and one of the good-looking boys had hazel eyes.

"I'm K-Ci, and that's my brother Jo-Jo."

"I'm Devante," said the one with the hazel eyes.

"I'm Devante's brother, Dalvin," said the other handsome one.

"And who's that?" I asked, pointing at the fifth person in the bunch.

"He's our cousin," one of the brothers said.

"Are y'all a new group signed to Uptown?" I asked.

"Yes, ma'am. We just met with Andre at the other office."

"Really?"

"Yes, ma'am. We are driving back to North Carolina and stopped here first to meet the rest of the staff."

"The rest of the staff is downstairs, that way," I said, pointing to the spiral staircase.

"I'm staying up here with you," Dalvin said as the others trotted down the stairs.

Dalvin pulled up a chair and sat down beside me, and I instantly felt a connection to him. By the time the rest of his band members were ready to hit the road again, Dalvin had practically talked my ears off.

"Here's my business card," Dalvin said to me as they prepared to walk out the front door. "Call me."

"Okay," I said while examining his homemade business card.

Spring 1989

The two sets of brothers were back in the Big Apple, but this time to stay. They were ready to embark on a new career—one that would ultimately take them around the world as one of the most memorable R&B groups of all time: Jodeci.

Before that moment arrived, though, Dalvin, Devante, K-Ci, JoJo, and their cousin met me at the Brooklyn office early Sunday morning, May 21, 1989. I will never forget the date. How could I? It was on my 27th birthday.

Sandra, the office manager, was supposed to meet them, but she didn't want to spend her off day babysitting, so she asked me to go in her stead since I happened to be living nearby at the YWCA of Brooklyn, which was within walking distance. I agreed. But, even if I'd lived a million miles away, I would've still said yes.

When I turned up at the office around nine or so in the morning, Jodeci was packed in a van in front of the building. They'd been parked out there all night long, they told me.

Once inside, Dalvin was back in my face to pick up where he'd last left off and trust me when I say I had no objections; the young boy was fine as hell, and I was excited to be in his company, too.

"Why didn't you call me, Vanessa?" he asked.

"I don't know."

Andre arrived around noon to take the boys to their new abode, so we all hopped into the two whips parked out front. Devante and I rode with Andre in his black Jeep, and the rest of the fellows rode in the van they'd driven from Charlotte.

When we pulled up in front of a Housing Projects in the Bronx, I must admit I was taken aback. For some reason, I expected a big, fancy house somewhere in New Jersey. What was I thinking?

The guys unloaded their luggage from the van, then we made our way inside a pissy elevator that took us up to an untidy apartment, an apartment that once upon a time housed Andre and his family.

After we took a quick tour around their new dwelling, we all ended up in one of the small bedrooms. Dalvin grabbed one of his bags and proceeded to empty the contents onto the floor.

"Wait, Dalvin!" I said. "Let me sweep up this trash before you dump all those sneakers on the floor."

While I swept up dust bunnies and reefer butts with a broom I'd found in the kitchen, Andre gave the guys a little pep talk.

"Are you all going to be okay?" Andre asked them at the end of his talk.

"Yes, sir! We'll be just fine with Vanessa here with us," Dalvin blurted out.

"Good. I'm out," said Andre.

"Do y'all have money for food?" I asked the guys as Andre walked out of the bedroom.

"No," they responded in unison.

"Andre, hol' up!" I yelled, catching up with him before he reached the front door. "Can you leave some money, so they can get something to eat? They don't have any food here, you know."

Andre dug in his pants pocket, pulled out a twenty-dollar bill, and handed it to me, then zoomed out the front door.

"Andre gave me twenty bucks so y'all can get something to eat," I said. "What do y'all want from the store?"

"Bring back a six-pack of beer," Devante said.

"What kind?"

"Heineken."

Dalvin and I left the apartment to find the nearest grocery store, where we bought the beer and some other food items and snacks, then jetted back to the crib. Devante snatched the six-pack from my hands and moved toward one of the bedrooms, where Jo-Jo, K-Ci, and their cousin were lounging the night away.

"Wait a minute!" I said before Devante could get away. "Let me get a beer." I cracked open my beer, took a couple swallows, then sat on Dalvin's lap on the living room sofa. "You don't want a beer, Dalvin?" I asked, not realizing he was only 17 years old—just two months shy of his 18th birthday.

"No, I don't drink."

I was enjoying Dalvin's company so much that by the time I checked my watch, it was way past midnight, and the house was quiet, except for Dalvin. He had stories for hours on end, and some of his stories required a few karate chops and kicks to the air.

Eventually, I excused myself and headed to the bathroom, only to find Devante lying on the floor. "Ohmygod!" I squealed. "Are you alive?" I nudged him with my foot. He didn't budge, but he let out a low moan that told me he'd drank too much beer.

"Dalvin!" I yelled from the bathroom. "Your brother is passed out on the bathroom floor, and I gots to pee."

"Step over him," Dalvin yelled back.

"But he's lying right in front of the toilet." I tried pushing Devante to one side, but he was like dead weight. "Dalvin!" I yelled again. "Let's pick him up and put him in bed."

"No! Leave him there."

I could no longer hold in my urine, so I somehow managed to lift my mini jean skirt to my waist, slide down my panties, sit my butt on the toilet seat and quickly handled my scandal. After I washed my hands, I made my way back to the living room and crashed on the couch alongside Dalvin until the sun rose.

When I got up to leave, I checked the bathroom first. Yup. Devante was still sleeping on the bathroom floor.

I found my way to the nearest train station, and before long, I was back at the YWCA with just enough time to shower and change before I was due at the office to answer my first phone call of the day.

Monday, May 22, 1989.

Ring...ring...ring.

"Good morning. Uptown. This is Vanessa. How may I direct your call?"

"Hey, Vanessa. Dis Dalvin. I'm coming down to the office to hang out with you."

"Okay. See you when you get here."

CHAPTER 13

My plan was to slowly work my way up the ladder, one step at a time, while learning all the ins and outs of the music game; however, a few months after my start date that plan drastically changed.

Ring…ring…ring.

"Good morning. Uptown. This is Vanessa. How may I direct your call?"

"Vanessa, this is Andre. What up, money?"

"Ain't nothin' up."

"Vanessa, you're not the receptionist anymore."

"Huh?"

I was puzzled. I knew I was doing an excellent job. I was doing above and beyond the call of duty. Andre had told me himself I was doing great; so why was he taking my job away from me? I loved my job.

That's when it dawned on me: Leslie, a young pretty girl who'd come to the office, unsuspectedly, about thirty minutes before Andre's call, was there to replace me.

Thirty minutes earlier

"Hi, how can I help you?" I asked Leslie after opening the front door for her.

"I work here now," Leslie replied as she plopped her petite frame into a chair in the reception area.

"You work here? Right now?"

"Yup. Andre hired me."

"He hired you to do what?"

"I don't know."

"What do you know how to do?"

"Nothing. I ain't worked in over ten years."

The only job that required knowing nothing or very little was my job. I asked each employee if they knew about Leslie; they all said no. Leslie made absolutely no sense, which told me something underhanded was taking place. I questioned her some more, but the only other information I got from her before Andre hit me up to set the record straight was that she was the sister of one of Andre's girlfriends, Wendy Credle, former A&R executive for MCA Records, now an entertainment lawyer.

"You're the publicist now," Andre continued, breaking through my thoughts. "I want you to train Leslie to be a great receptionist like you. And by the way, I'm taking you out to lunch tomorrow."

After he told me he had also increased my salary to an extra $5,000 annually, he hung up. After that kind of phone call, one would suspect I'd be elated—so, why wasn't I?

Bucky Whitehead, general manager and in-house lawyer, wasn't thrilled, either; as a matter of fact, he was fuming mad when Andre phoned him, straight after speaking to me, to inform him that I was now the new Director of Publicity. Bucky slammed down the phone and trotted his tall, dark, goofy-self up the spiral stairs, giving me the evil eye behind his bifocals before storming out the front door.

As far as Bucky was concerned, I didn't deserve such a position because, unlike him, I didn't go to Yale and Columbia Law School. So, in his eyes, I was nothing more than a two-bit, uneducated ghetto girl who had no rights in that type of capacity, and he made sure to remind me and others of that.

Furthermore, he'd promised Zipporah (one of his lady friends) the publicist position was hers and when she saw me in passing at the Manhattan office, she had no qualms about telling me, with a nasty attitude, "You stole my job!"

Before my promotion, Bucky and I had become ace boon coons after he'd hired me to be the receptionist, and we'd hang out quite often during and after work. Although he'd tell me often that I was ghetto, he enjoyed being around this ghetto girl. It didn't surprise me, though. Most cornballs find me exciting and the life of their corny party.

But the feelings were mutual. I enjoyed his company, too, so it saddened me to know that he didn't wish me well in my new endeavor. He wanted me to remain in his nest, under his control, until he decided I could fly higher and whereto. After all, he was the one who brought me onboard, and so he didn't appreciate Andre going behind his back to promote me, his protégé, especially when he'd told Andre not to.

He didn't like the fact that I was now under Andre's wing, which meant he could no longer give me directives, which he greatly enjoyed. Andre had stolen me from him, and his jealousy was so strong, I could smell it seeping through his pores.

The next day, I hooked up with Andre at the Manhattan office; then he and I walked to a nearby Japanese restaurant to celebrate my new position. As I sat across from Andre, I thought about telling him how uncomfortable I felt taking on this job as the head of the publicity department.

I'd really wanted to start off as the assistant to a publicist, which was why weeks prior, when I knew Andre was considering hiring a publicist, I'd suggested he hire one of my friends, Nathasha Brooks-Harris, now Doctor Nathasha Brooks-Harris. I thought she'd make a great publicist for Uptown because at the time she was working as a freelance writer.

Andre seemed so excited about being able to give me this great opportunity, so I said nothing; instead, I just sipped on my glass of red wine and ate the sushi I'd ordered while Andre made small talk before asking me a personal question.

"Do your children have the same father?"

"Yes."

I wondered why it mattered to him whether my children had the same father, but I didn't ask.

After lunch, we hopped in a yellow cab Andre flagged down. I had no idea where we were going next. Ten minutes later, we ended up in a jewelry store.

For a quick second, I got happy thinking Andre was going to buy me diamonds to go along with my new position. That was hardly the case. Andre simply wanted to exchange his $9,000 watch for a $10,000 watch.

"What's wrong with that watch?" I asked Andre while pointing at the $9,000 watch on his wrist.

"It's too gaudy."

I noticed Andre glanced down at my left wrist through his bifocals, so I quickly moved it behind my back to hide the eighty-dollar gold-plated watch wrapped around it, not to mention, the worn-out, poor quality ensemble I was clad in as I stood next to my 29-year-old, handsome, nerdy-looking, chubby boss kitted out in a dark-colored Armani type suit and pocket hanky over an expensive looking shirt, formal ascot tie knotted at his throat. Yup! He was dressed to the nines, and I was dressed like a bum…well, that's how I felt—inferior.

As Andre paid the extra G for his new watch, I thought about all the things I could've bought with ten grand, other than a watch. I thought about a down payment for a nice home for my children who were still in my mother's care at my aunt's place.

The next day, the members of Jodeci stopped by the Brooklyn office. They congratulated me on my new position, and as usual, Dalvin was showing me love and affection. Then they all headed downstairs to Bucky's office.

Shortly after, JoJo ran back upstairs and pulled me to the side and asked, "Who did you sleep with to get this job?" As my body stiffened at the offensive remark, JoJo answered his own question. "You slept with Bucky."

"I did not!"

"Yes, you did."

"I did not!"

"Yes, you did! You know how I know?"

"How?"

"Because Bucky told us something about you."

"What did he say?"

"I'm not telling you. But I know you had sex with him because of what he said about you."

Instead of storming down the spiral stairs to confront cockblocking Bucky about this matter, I simply sucked my teeth and rolled my eyes at JoJo, realizing there was nothing I could say to convince him that I'd never had sexual intercourse with Bucky.

This was the same thing that happened when I was 15; nothing I said was going to convince my second boyfriend that I was a virgin who had not slept with a bunch of boys as my jealous best friend had claimed.

Further, if I was a loose hoochie-coochie, I would've smashed Dalvin, who by the way, was heated at the thought that I was covertly letting Bucky knock my screws loose while he was in the process of trying to be my man. Dalvin was so upset at that disturbing news, he went running back to Charlotte, and he and I didn't speak to each other until he returned to New York a couple weeks later. Unfortunately, the power of Bucky's words had changed the dynamic of my relationship with Dalvin as Bucky had hoped.

I brushed off JoJo's false accusations and wondered what in the heck was I going to do in my new role as Uptown's publicist. In my own eyes, I lacked everything needed to pull off this skyscraping gig. I didn't have one of those strong, assertive personalities, and I didn't stand up to folk who'd crossed the line with me; instead, I allowed them to piss all over me and I didn't set any boundaries.

Besides that, I didn't even have nice clothes to at least look the part. I wasn't articulate as I imagined a publicist should be, and to top it all off, I had no public relations experience.

If all the King's horses and all the King's men couldn't put Humpty Dumpty back together again, then how could the items in my bag of tricks turn me into a well-informed publicist overnight when the only thing I knew about publicists was that they had arranged for me to interview recording artists during my tenure at *Class Magazine*?

Prior, I'd never even heard the word publicist. Oh, yea. There's one other thing I learned about publicists, they threw nice parties. At least Simo Doe did.

CHAPTER 14

Simo Doe was the publicist for Atlantic Records. I was her favorite contact person when I worked at *Class Magazine*—or at least that's how she made me feel. She always contacted me whenever she wanted a write-up on one of Atlantic Records' hottest recording artists. She also made it her business to offer me invitations, be it a party, concert, or function.

Furthermore, when she'd witness me behaving like a groupie, which slipped out occasionally, she didn't hesitate to give me good motherly advice: "Vanessa," she'd say, "if you want to last in the music business, don't do that again!"

I appreciated her frankness and constructive criticism. She was a tad uppity but real, and I liked that about her—the real part. I liked her style, too. She was professional and sophisticated and always well-dressed, not to mention she was easy on the eyes with her beautiful long hair. That's the kind of publicist I wanted to be someday—when the time was right. Unfortunately, time and opportunity wait for no one.

I vividly remembered the party Simo threw for Miki Howard, one of Atlantic Records' artists. The party was for the release of Miki's debut album, *Come Share My Love*, which happened to be one of my all-time favorite albums. It was held November 19, 1986, at Stringfellows, a New York City nightclub located in Manhattan on 21st Street.

I carefully observed the way Simo stood at the door and greeted each invited guest, many of whom she knew by name. I remembered the way she made me feel as I walked through that door and was greeted by her 'happy to see you' smile. She made me feel special, like I was somebody important, as she welcomed me into the club and handed me a wonderfully made small shopping bag filled with Miki Howard promotional items.

Once inside the club, Miki spotted me and walked up beside me. She must've sensed that I was feeling a tad salty at the way she'd slighted me earlier that day; so, she seized my hand, then asked me if I wanted to grab a seat at one of the tables so that she and I could continue the conversation we'd had a few hours before her party.

Before my Higher-Self had a chance to gladly accept her invitation, and maybe even gain a new friend in her, my lower-self, my stupid ego, quickly jumped into the conversation and with attitude, said, "No! I got my story!"

Earlier that day, November 19, 1986

Simo arranged an interview between me and Miki Howard. "Meet us at the Sheraton at four o'clock," she told me over the phone.

When I arrived at a downtown Manhattan Sheraton hotel, Simo introduced me to Miki, who was sitting at a table in the hotel's restaurant in the lobby area. Right after our introduction, Simo exited the building.

As I joined Miki at her table, a waiter brought over a pot of tea she'd ordered prior to my arrival. She had on a wrinkled shirt, slacks, and—if I'm not mistaken—slippers, or what looked like slippers. Her hair was untidy, and she wore no make-up. She looked like she'd just awakened. Still, she looked stunning.

"You want some tea?" she asked me.

"Yeah, thank you," I said. I grabbed a cup and poured tea into it, then I added a couple scoops of sugar and gave my tea a stir before taking a sip.

"Come on! Come on! Hurry up!" Miki snapped.

She seemed anxious to get back to her room, so I quickly put the cup of tea down and reached inside my purse, whipped out my sixty-dollar machine, pressed record, then threw out some questions that she civilly and quickly answered. Then, just like Doug E. Fresh, Miki had a question of her own to ask me.

"How old are you?"

"Twenty-four."

"What?" she exclaimed. "You're my age! I thought you were a high school kid."

"Yeah, I get that a lot."

After I told her I was a mother of two, too, I was able to squeeze in one more question before, out of the blue, she jumped out of her seat. "I gotta go," she said as she kissed my neck, of all places, then she jetted off into the nearby elevator.

Left all alone at the table, feeling stupid, I took a few more sips of my tea and wondered, who's responsible for this tab? Did she already pay up front? Was it added to her hotel tab? What was the protocol?

I had no clue, but whatever it was, I knew I wasn't going to pay for all that tea, nor was I about to leave a tip. I couldn't if I wanted to. My pockets were bare, except for my one and only token to ride the C train back to my rat-infested Washington Heights apartment, where I was residing at the time.

I looked around the room and saw the waiter who'd served the tea. He was a tall, dark-haired, young white guy. While he was paying attention to another customer across the room, I decided that there was no better time than now to flee, in case I was responsible for the bill.

I quietly got up and calmly walked toward the entrance, looking straight ahead, hoping I didn't get that tap on the shoulder and, "Excuse me, Miss, you forgot to pay."—whew!

CHAPTER 15

In my new position as head of the publicity department, I did nothing except drift around sadly as self-doubt and fear overwhelmed me to the point of paralysis.

Who was going to teach me how to be this top-notch publicist Andre had imagined I'd be? I suggested shadowing Simo Doe, but Andre wasn't feeling her. He suggested I follow and observe Juanita Stephens, publicist for MCA Records. "She has more experience with rappers," he told me.

Thus, Andre planned for me to hook up with Juanita. I attended one photo shoot she'd arranged for Heavy D and the Boyz and for the most part, she ignored me.

The next day, I popped up at her office to shadow her again, and just like the day before, she practically ignored me. To make matters worse, the next day a co-worker whispered in my ear, "Juanita told me she doesn't want you watching her work."

That was all I needed to hear. I never went around Juanita again. Besides, I was trying to emulate Simo Doe: classy, kind, professional, and eager to share her knowledge.

As the weeks went by, I continued to do absolutely nothing. I had no one to train me, and Andre never gave me any assignments. I was left to figure it out on my own.

There came a point when I'd call out sick, something I'd never done when I was the receptionist. I just didn't feel comfortable sitting in the small upstairs office, twiddling my thumbs all day, while staring at Doug E. Fresh posters.

I grew increasingly disconsolate, and my negative thoughts began overpowering my positive ones. Once a go-getter brimming with self-assurance, I'd somehow lost my magic and turned into a pancake, flipping from Miss Happy-Go-Lucky to Miss Chicken-Butt. It was apparent to others that I wasn't the same bubbly hustler before my promotion, that sweet, young, cheerful woman who'd somehow convinced Andre I was right for the job.

He was correct, nonetheless. I was right for the job even with the little knowledge I had about publicity. There was enough information to get the job done, but I didn't know my worth, and my fear-self, unfortunately, wouldn't stop whispering in my ears: "You're stupid. You can't even articulate. You're ghetto. How are you 'pose to speak on behalf of the artists with that ghetto dialect...dummy!"

I felt like Sissy Spacek in the movie *Carrie* when her character tells her religious-fanatic mother she wants to go to the prom. Her mother scolds her and says, "They're all gonna laugh at you!"

What bothered me most of all, however, was that I let Andre down. In due course, I wanted to make him proud of me the way Mary J. Blige and Puffy had made him proud; instead, I made him look like an idiot for promoting me. He was an idiot, some may say, but idiot or not, he was simply trying to take me to a higher level in the music game because he saw something in me that I didn't see in myself; he saw the part of me that had the potential to evolve into something great and top-notch and for that, I would be forever grateful. But right then, I was sorry it wasn't working out.

CHAPTER 16

While I was failing miserably as the company's publi-cist, Puffy was quickly soaring in his new position as head of the A&R department. If I didn't know any better, I'd swear he stole my magician's robe and my bag of tricks.

Puffy was a flashy-dresser with an outgoing personality, and we hit it off fast.

"Vanessa, can you write a bio for me?" he asked one day while I was the underpaid receptionist and he was an intern.

"What for?"

"I'm a dancer. I'm in a dance group."

He must've heard through the wire that I had written articles that were published in magazines.

"Nope. I'm not gonna do it, Puffy. I'm not doing nothing no more except answer the phone."

"Come on, Vanessa. Pleassse."

"Nope! I'm not doing nothing else extra around here until Andre pays me more money."

I still remember the day Heavy D had a party at his home in Mount Vernon. It was during the springtime, a few days after my 27th birthday. I had never been to Mount Vernon, nor did I have a clue as to how I was going to get there.

"I'll take you to the party," a tall dark man announced. He was a wannabe who had unexpectantly popped up at the Brooklyn office to see Bucky. Even though I didn't have the foggiest idea who he was, the only thing that mattered at that moment was that the brother had a car, and I had a party to attend.

I contacted Dalvin and told him that I had gotten us a ride to Heavy's party. I told him to gather up his bandmates and meet me at the Manhattan office on 57th Street.

"We don't have money to get down there," Dalvin said.

"Hop the train, then."

"What if we get caught?"

"Y'all are going to jail if you get caught, so please don't get caught."

Yes, I felt bad advising them to turnstile-jump, but that was how everybody I knew did it when short on cash; it was the New York way. Thankfully, they pulled it off. The last thing I needed was for them to end up in jail because of my bad advice.

When the wannabe and I pulled up in front of Uptown's Manhattan office building in his small raggedy Yugo, I wasn't expecting to see Puffy, too, standing in front of the building. How in the heck are seven people going to fit in this miniature vehicle? I pondered.

Dalvin sat up front with me and the driver, of course. Puffy and the other three members of Jodeci tried with all their might to squeeze in the back seat, unsuccessfully. Somebody was going to have to crouch down in the car's storage compartment or trunk, and it was looking like it was going to have to be the smallest one out of the bunch.

When I looked over my shoulder and saw that Puffy had secured his thin frame a spot in the back seat, I knew it wasn't going to be him, either; plus, he wasn't the smallest.

On the ride to Mount Vernon, we all giggled when we caught a glimpse of K-Ci curled up like a newborn baby in the tiny storage compartment, protesting the whole way.

When we arrived at Heavy's house, Dalvin and I entered the party hand in hand as if we were a couple. On our way to the backyard, we saw a small crowd in a room leading to the yard. We stopped to see what had their attention.

It was Run (DMC) giving a sermon. After a few seconds of listening to him, we realized he was incoherent, rambling, so we kept it moving to the backyard where Andre and a bunch of other guests were.

While I was huddled in a circle with Puffy and all the members of Jodeci, Andre approached us.

"Vanessa," he said, "introduce them to Eddie F." (Eddie F was Heavy D's DJ and one of his producers.)

"I did already," I said.

"That's why I like you, Vanessa," Puffy chimed in. "You're just like me: a go-getter."

And just like me, Puffy caught Andre's attention, too. Just like me, Puff showed up at nearly every New York City industry party. And, when possible, he even made it his business to walk into a party on the arms of a famous person in hopes of landing in a magazine or two alongside the public figure—e.g., Rosie Perez.

Flashforward: Summer 1989

Puffy walked on the red carpet leading to the club, locked arm in arm with Rosie Perez. She was the co-star of Spike Lee's movie: *Do the Right Thing*, and tonight was the movie's afterparty at a New York City club. I was already inside the club, standing near the club's entrance, chopping it up with Teddy Riley, whom I'd just introduced myself to before Flavor Flav appeared out of nowhere and jumped in-between Teddy and me. "FLAVOR FLAVVVVVVV!!!" he yelled, startling the crap out of me.

I'd never met Flav in person before this moment, so, my first impression of him...let's just say, I was so thankful Puffy spotted me during that awkwardly, scary, brief period of time. He released Rosie's arm to run into mine and gave me a 'happy-to-see-you' hug before he ran back to his date.

I spotted Fab 5 Freddy, former host of YO! MTV Raps, and quickly walked toward him, leaving Teddy Riley with that nut.

Fab and I had met weeks prior, thanks to Andre Harrell who introduced us. I found him to be one of the coolest, down-to-earth persons in the entertainment game. Every time he'd see me, he'd greet me with a big hug as if he was happy to see and know me.

Since I was the new publicist for Uptown Records, Fab thought I should get to know Jamie Foster Brown, owner and publisher of *Sister 2 Sister Magazine* (now folded), which, at the time, was a recent developed African-American magazine some categorized the black *People Magazine*.

Fab and I sauntered over to where Jamie was standing all alone, then Fab said to her, "Hi Jamie, I want to introduce you to Vanessa, Uptown Record's new publicist."

"Hello," I said. "Nice to meet you."

Jamie took one quick look at me, turned up her high-falutin-yellow nose, then looked away from us. Fab and I looked at each other and I knew we were thinking the same thing: Cuckoo. After we snapped out of our punch-drunk state, we walked away from her.

Rewind: Heavy D's Party

After Puff expressed his admiration for me in the backyard at Heavy's party, he convinced and coached Jodeci to sing happy birthday to Hev, acapella. Later, we spotted Salt.

"Oooo, I want to meet her," Dalvin begged me. "I love Salt N Pepa."

Even though I didn't know her personally, I knew her man, Hurby Azor. Purple and I met him back when we were contestants at the beauty pageant where we'd met the

Audio Two. Hurby was friends with the man in charge of the pageant who'd introduced us to Hurby.

Hurby had promised to make me and Purple famous rappers like Salt N Pepa. So, we were always hanging out with him at parties or some of his artists' studio sessions or his house. He introduced us to Salt once at a party, then quickly snatched us away from her, giving us no time to even become her acquaintance.

Anyway, I introduced Dalvin to Salt; afterward, she turned to me and said, "Don't I know you from somewhere?"

I didn't want to get into a conversation with her about Hurby or about the time my friend, Elaine Woods (now known as Mrs. Elaine Swann, Lifestyle and Etiquette Expert), and I met her at a New York City club under a not so good situation.

"Look, Vanessa!" Elaine said as she entered a stall in the ladies' room at the club. "Someone lost their wallet."

"Is there any money in it?"

Elaine picked up the wallet and opened it. Inside there was nothing but the owner's photo ID card. "You're not going to believe whose wallet this is!"

"Who?"

"This is Salt's wallet!"

"Salt? Salt N Pepa?"

"Yes."

"Let's go find her and give it to her."

Elaine and I searched the club and saw Salt standing all alone. We approached her.

"We found this in the bathroom," Elaine said as she handed Salt the wallet.

"Thank you," Salt said as she grabbed the wallet. Then she looked inside. "I had a thousand dollars in it. I just took the thousand out the bank right before I came here. I knew I shouldn't have done that. My fault."

Elaine and I didn't know what to say to her after finding out someone stole her money. Does she think we stole it? We told her there was no money in it when we found it, but still, I think she believed we were the culprits, and so, when at Heavy's party she asked if she knew me from somewhere, I said, "No. I don't think so."

At the end of the night, the wannabe drove everyone home, except Puffy who resided in Mount Vernon, too; so, he stayed at Heavy's party—good news for K-Ci, who didn't have to ride in the trunk again.

The next day or so, Puffy called me at the Brooklyn office and told me he wanted company business cards with his name printed on them. "You gotta talk to Bucky about that," I told him. "Good luck."

I transferred the call to Bucky, who was working downstairs in his office. Apparently, Bucky didn't approve of an intern having company business cards the same way he didn't want me to be the company's publicist, and so, I had to listen to him bitch about Puffy and those damn business cards all day long.

I don't even know if Puffy got those cards while an intern. I doubt it. But I'm certain he did upon his rise to the A&R seat.

CHAPTER 17

A few months had passed since my promotion and instead of managing the spread of information like a publicist is supposed to do, I was still walking around zombified. Andre knew he had to do something about my lack of enthusiasm, but what?

He eventually went with the idea of setting up a fake all-employee evaluation day to be held in the boardroom at the Manhattan office. No one had to tell me; I knew this day was made exclusively for me, but I played the dumb role as if I didn't know it was the day I'd be set free from my job as a deadbeat publicist.

When it was my turn to enter the boardroom for my fake evaluation, I overheard some of my co-workers whispering and laughing at me as I walked past them with my head held down. Then, one of them chanted out loud, "Somebody's getting fired! Somebody's getting fired!"

Inside the conference room, I sat at a long cherry wood table amid Andre Harrell, Bucky Whitehead, and Steve Lucas (another executive). For the first time since my big promotion, I didn't feel butterflies swimming around in my stomach. I felt relieved. I knew my high-powered position was finally over, but Andre didn't seem to know how to tell me.

They all sat quietly at the table, looking stupid, until Bucky, who'd irked my nerves since the day I got promoted, made a few silly comments. I stared him down for a good, long minute, then rolled my eyes at him.

"She's insubordinate!" he cried out, obviously forgetting I didn't work for him nor under him.

I shook my head at him before turning my attention to Andre. "You talk," I said. "You're the boss."

"I want you to be my assistant," Andre said, completely ignoring Bucky's silly outcry. "but you probably don't even like me."

"I like you," I replied without hesitating. "I want to be your assistant."

"Okay. I want you to start tomorrow," Andre said. "Be here at ten o'clock."

"Tomorrow?" I cried out. "Elaine Woods and I made plans to be in Atlanta, Georgia tomorrow for the Jack the Rapper convention. Can I start when we get back?"

"No! You can't go to Jack the Rapper. I want you here tomorrow at ten o'clock, and don't be late!"

I was a little bummed about not being able to go to Atlanta, Georgia for the first time. Elaine and I had spent all week planning the trip, and now she'd have to go by herself.

I felt terrible that I couldn't join her as we had planned. Oh well, at least I was still an Uptown employee and as far as I was concerned, Jack the Rapper couldn't beat that.

My new position as the executive assistant to the CEO of Uptown Records came with another raise, which left me wondering whether I'd been demoted or promoted. My new job title told me I had been demoted, but my pay raise said otherwise.

I'd finally copped my own apartment, too—sort of. An associate of mine, Michael Fisher, offered to sublet his apartment to me. It was a one-bedroom basement apartment in a brownstone on Bergen Street, in downtown Brooklyn, minutes from the Barclay Center—which didn't exist then.

"Six-fifty per month, and it's all yours," Michael said.

"Don't I have to sign a lease?" I asked Michael.

"No. Not right now."

Ding...ding...ding! My spidey senses began beeping and tingling at the thought of not signing a lease; but, who in their right mind pays attention to their intuition all the time?

So, I got my children from Millie, who was still living with her sister and we moved in. I enrolled them in a nearby public school and carried on in my new position as Andre's assistant until I got a phone call that altered the course of my life.

I was on the phone with Elaine when the call came in. "Hold on, Elaine; that's my other line," I said.

"Vanessa, this is Andre."

My heart sank to the floor. I knew why he was calling. It was a Thursday evening, and I'd not reported to work since last Friday.

"Hi, Andre. What's up?"

"I'm letting you go, Vanessa."

"Why?" I asked, trying to sound clueless.

"You're not doing what I want you to do. I didn't give you permission to take a vacation."

"I know, but I needed one. I left you a note stating that I would be on vacation for a week. I never took a vacation day. I was coming back to work on Monday."

"I'll tell you what: you can go back to being the receptionist at the Brooklyn office, and I'm reducing your salary."

"Uh, no, Andre. I can't do that."

"Okay. Then you can pick up your severance pay tomorrow at the Brooklyn office."

Going all the way back down to the receptionist at the Brooklyn office meant going back to work under Bucky's wings, and to me that would be equivalent to going back to live with an abusive, narcissistic boyfriend whose wishes better be my command, or else there would be hell to pay.

Not only that, who at the company would respect me after tumbling all the way down the ladder after being handed an opportunity of a lifetime and screwing it all up? In the words of Keith Sweat: Nobody!

Devastated. I clicked back over to see if Elaine was still on the other line. Yup, she sure was. Too distraught to continue my conversation with her, I gave her a lame excuse about why I had to end the call.

The next day, my children and I walked to the Brooklyn office to pick up my severance pay. Along with my check, Bucky was delighted to hand me a memo, that he'd typed up, that stated that I was terminated as if Andre hadn't already told me. That big self-satisfying grin on his face told me just how happy he was.

As I was preparing to leave, another employee approached me to tell me that Andre had hired a white girl to replace me and he was paying her twice the amount he'd paid me.

"And she's got her own personal assistant, too," the employee told me.

From the Brooklyn office, I strolled on over to Hoyt and Schermerhorn to the nearest unemployment office. Once that matter was squared away, my children and I hopped on the A train, which took us to East Village, where we had lunch at BBQ's.

The next week, a temp agency found me a job as a typist at a small black-owned accounting firm in Bedford-Stuyvesant. A week later, I convinced the owner of the accountant firm to eliminate the temp agency and pay me directly, under the table. The arrangement worked out well for both me and the employer.

CHAPTER 18

Ring...ring...ring.

"Hello?"

"Hi, Vanessa. This is Tajuna."

Tajuna Sharpe was Bucky's newly appointed assistant, thanks to me for advising him to hire her instead of the other candidate, when he'd asked me, during my tenure as the receptionist, "Which one should I hire?"

Tajuna had replaced Sandra Zuniga who'd been promoted to work under Jimmy "Luv" Jenkins, another executive who ran the promotions department.

"What's up, girl?" I asked Tajuna.

"Bucky asked me to call you because he didn't have the guts to tell you himself."

"Tell me what?"

"He asked Sandy first, but she didn't want to tell you, either."

"Tell me what?"

"Do not show up at Uptown's party tomorrow."

"Why?"

"Bucky said Andre doesn't want you there and if you show up, Andre's going to have security escort you out of the building."

"Really? Okay. Thanks for letting me know, Tajuna."

Something was very odd about that message. I never told anyone I was going to attend Uptown's party. Aside from that, Andre and I were on good terms, but Bucky obviously wasn't aware of that. If he was, he'd have never made up that outlandish story.

What Bucky didn't know was that Andre and I had a very positive and pleasant run-in at another party given by Elaine, to promote her modeling agency: Petite Models. Her party was held days before Uptown's party.

The special guest scheduled to perform at Elaine's party was an Uptown recording artist named Jeff Redd. He was the reason Andre was at Elaine's party. When I spotted Andre, I went over to the bar to greet him. His face lit up with joy. After we embraced, he thanked me from the bottom of his heart for the nice card I had mailed to his home immediately following my dismissal from Uptown. It was a thank-you-for-the-opportunity card.

So, when Tajuna relayed that message to me, I knew it didn't come from Andre. He had no motive, but Bucky, the green-eyed goofy monster, did.

CHAPTER 19

I didn't attend Uptown's party. And Michael Fisher, my so-called landlord, who'd sublet his apartment to me, somehow heard through the rumor mill that I was no longer an Uptown employee, and so, he phoned me right away on a cold, blustery Sunday evening.

"Why didn't you tell me you were fired?"

I was taken aback by the hostility in his tone; it was a tone I'd never met. If the tone of his voice could kill, I'd be dead right now; it sounded as if I had betrayed him by losing my job since I happen to be his connection to Uptown Records.

I didn't know it till then, but Michael was one of those fake friends. You know the kind: the ones who befriend you because of your connection to something, then, when you're no longer connected to that something, drop you like a hot potato.

"I want my apartment back!" he yelled.

"Why?" I asked. "I just paid the rent, Michael."

"Why didn't you tell me you got fired? I want you out right now!"

"I'm not leaving now!" I shouted back. "It's dark and cold outside!"

"Who do you think you're talking to like that?" he yelled before slamming down the phone; then, within minutes, he was banging on my door which was actually his door because he had the lease to the apartment and I had nothing but my word against his; so, I let him in hoping to rectify this situation that made absolutely no sense to me. Once inside, the yelling continued.

"I want you out! Now!"

My children didn't understand his anger problem, either. Their facial expressions said, "Why is this six-foot-plus giant yelling at Mommy?" My fragile 10-year-old daughter, who always became traumatized any time she saw an argument or fight pop off, cried a river as Michael ranted and raved; her tears of fear didn't faze him one iota.

After I refused to leave, Michael left. Thinking the coast was clear, I decided to wash the dirty dishes, so, I turned on the faucet and to my horror, the water was scalding. I immediately phoned the alleged culprit.

"What did you do to the water?" I yelled through the phone at Michael. "What is your problem, you big dummy?"

"I want you out!" He yelled before slamming down the phone…again; then, within minutes, the apartment went black. Soon after, I heard a loud banging on my door…I mean Michael's door. I knew it was him, but considering I'd never seen him in possession of a car, I wondered how he was able to get to me so quickly even though he did live within walking distance. Still, he must've ran or maybe he never went home and had been hiding around the corner the whole time. I didn't know. All I knew was he was straight tripping; so, I did not let him in this time.

"Turn the lights back on, or I'm calling the police!" I yelled through the door.

He turned on the lights but in the face of his unusual behavior, I called the police anyways. They arrived within minutes, probably because my zip code revealed I was living in a predominately white neighborhood.

Michael was already outside when the officers arrived, so he greeted the two white boys in blue first. I peered through the blinds and watched Michael as he spoke to the officers for a good ten minutes or so; that was a bad sign. I knew Michael, a white man himself, who'd studied law and attended the same prestigious university as Bucky, would make a better impression on them than I would.

Okay, okay, okay! Michael's not pure white, just for the record. However, his white German side was more noticeable than his black side; so much so that if he wanted to join the KKK or participate in an alt-right rally, let's just say, he'd have absolutely no problem blending in.

When the officers finally came inside the apartment to talk to me, I told them I was the one who'd initially called them, and that I didn't appreciate them talking to Michael first. As I proceeded to tell my side of the story, one of the officers cut me off and told me I had to vacate the premises. They clearly had no interest in what I had to say. It didn't even matter to them. They were evidently assisting Michael with an illegal eviction.

"Miss," one of the white boys in blue told me. "you have to leave now."

"But I have nowhere to go," I replied. "Can I stay here until tomorrow?"

"I'm sorry, Miss. You need to vacate the premises now!"

"But where am I supposed to go at this time of night with two small children?"

"I don't know, Miss. Do you want us to take you to a shelter?"

"Yeah, okay, I guess."

What else was I supposed to say or do? I had no written rental contract; all I had was a verbal agreement between Michael and me, so it was my word against his. Also, I had no idea what story Michael had told the boys in blue. On top of that, I had neither the familiarity with nor the know-how to deal with law-related issues like this. It would be years later, while watching *The Judge Mathis Show*, I would come to learn I had a strong case against Michael, that I could have sued him for an illegal eviction and intentional infliction of emotional distress upon me and my children.

Not knowing exactly what to do at that moment, I phoned my friend, Dr. Nathasha Brooks-Harris, and told her everything that was transpiring.

"Where are you going?" she asked.

"The cops are taking us to a shelter."

"Oh, no! You don't want to go to a shelter, Vanessa. Those shelters are terrible. Come stay with me."

Nathasha's parents owned a big multi-family brownstone. She lived in one of the apartments in the brownstone. The brownstone was located in downtown Brooklyn, roughly ten minutes away from me—give or take; so, I called a cab and threw as many of our things into the trunk as I could fit at one time.

Michael and the boys in blue were standing outside watching. "I'll be right back to get a few more things," I told Michael before we hopped into the taxicab. I'd also asked him if I could hold on to the key until the next day, at which time I'd return with a U-Haul to get the bigger items and place them in storage. He agreed.

When we arrived at Nathasha's, we unloaded the taxi, put our things in her house, then jumped back in the cab to go back for more of our stuff. After we'd entered the gate that leads to the basement apartment, I noticed all of our belongings had been tossed on the floor in the hallway. I took my key out of my purse so I could unlock the front door to the apartment. To my surprise, a big ol' padlock was in front of the keyhole. And Michael...well, he was nowhere to be found.

I couldn't believe he was that heartless, especially since I'd never done anything bad to him. The only thing I'd ever done was invite him out to a couple of concerts and parties or let him wine and dine me.

We hung out often, and whenever we did, he'd tell me nosey Bucky had asked him if we'd had sex. Michael wasn't the only man that had informed me that Bucky had asked them if they'd had sex with me. But I digress.

Michael, on the other hand, seemed like a genuinely kind person and friend until I lost my job. His behavior toward me was shocking. So, that's when I began to wonder if this situation was much deeper than Michael, like maybe something in the invisible realms were orchestrating my Rise, Reign, and Fall.

First, I lost the job of my dreams, then I suffered an unlawful eviction, all within one month. Maybe this was the part of my journey where I get my big slice of humble pie, or maybe it was something I needed to experience before gaining clarity of my soul's purpose.

Whatever the case, those difficult encounters were humiliating. And it didn't make me feel any better when Nathasha, with well-intentions, of course, said, "I don't know what you did to deserve this, but you did something very bad."

I instantly felt like the Bible character, Job, whose friends tried to comfort him by accusing him of having done something terribly evil to deserve losing everything in one fell swoop.

Sometimes, I've come to learn, what may seem *bad* at the time may actually be for your highest good. Sometimes, all a person needs is a little perspective.

It was late, and I was too exhausted and stressed to deal with the big mess I was in and the big mess Michael left in the hallway. So, I told my children to look through the pile that Michael had made of our things and get anything important to them because I wasn't coming back there ever again. Whatever was left behind would stay left behind.

After my children grabbed a few of their belongings, we jumped back into the same cab and headed back to Nathasha's house. I was so done with that part of this mess I was in. I would deal with the other part in the morning.

The next morning, bright and early, my children and I arrived at Michael's apartment. It was time for me to deal with the other part of this mess: the rent money I'd paid Michael like two days before the illegal eviction.

"Unless you sign this," Michael warned me as he sat behind a desk in his apartment, "I am not giving you back your money!" He shoved a tiny torn-off piece of scrap paper at me. It was a handwritten contract that stated I wouldn't take legal action against him for evicting me.

"I'm not signing that!" I yelled.

Without a care in the world that two small children (10 and 7 years old) were in his presence and looking at him, Michael yelled back, "Unless you sign this, I'm not giving you your money!"

For a moment, I thought about contacting a few goons to manhandle him; luckily, I wasn't about that life, so I didn't know any goons.

I was mentally worn-out, though, and just simply wanted to be forever and completely done with Michael and this situation. So, under duress, I scribbled my name on that piece of paper. Of course, Michael didn't give me a copy, and quite frankly I didn't care. I was just happy this cycle was over.

We stayed with Nathasha for three weeks, then I got a call from my sister.

"Guess what?" she said, bursting with excitement.

"What?"

"I got accepted into the Projects!"

Hot damn! I got excited, too, if not more than her, even though we'd never discussed living together, but she knew, without question, mine and her predicament.

"When can we move in?" I asked.

My sister, Shell, told me it was going to take another week before New York City Housing Authority (NYCHA) gave her the key to her very first apartment. I knew the Most High's hand was wrapped up in this because that same day Nathasha, out of concern, I'm sure, asked me what my next move was going to be.

I assumed she wanted to know how much longer I planned to stay with her because I was sure I was wearing out my welcome, which is totally understandable. So, I asked her if I could stay one more week until my sister got the key. She agreed—Thanks, Nathasha!

What a glorious day for us all when a week later we moved into my sister's two-bedroom apartment at the Dyckman Housing Projects. We couldn't have cared less that we had to sleep on the floor for the first couple of weeks because there was no furniture in the apartment.

I ended up living with my sister for five months, then lo and behold, I, too, was accepted into my own two-bedroom, income-based apartment in Brooklyn. Now I, too, finally had my first real apartment.

Millie stayed with her sister a little while longer, then eventually she, too, was accepted into an income-based apartment in West Harlem. My brother—well, he was still incarcerated with baby daddy.

Several weeks after Uptown's party, another record label threw a party. Elaine contacted me and told me she was on the guest list and asked me to attend with her. While there, I spotted my former boss, Andre, across the room.

I was happy to see him, and he seemed happy to see me, too. So, I sauntered over to him and gave him a big bear hug. While I was cuddling him, Michael Fisher just so happened to walk past us. If you could've seen the look on Michael's face as he watched me hugged up on Andre... shocked silly best described it.

Andre noticed that Michael and I didn't speak to each other. "What's up with that?" Andre asked.

I briefly gave him the rundown about the illegal eviction, and then I asked Andre, "Did you say that you were going to have security escort me out of Uptown's party if I showed up?"

"I didn't say that! You can come to any party we have; you can even call me on my personal phone," Andre said. Then he popped the big question: "Do you want your high seat back, Vanessa?"

"High seat? What's a high seat?"

"My assistant. Do you want your job back as my assistant?"

I couldn't believe what I was hearing, even though, in the music industry, it's quite common for one to get fired and later rehired. Still, I wondered: is he serious? Is he really going to hire me back? I knew he was serious, but what about that white girl he'd hired to replace me? I wondered about that, too. And what about my current job at the black-owned accounting firm? I didn't want to walk out on them without notice. They were good to me.

I didn't know how to respond to Andre's offer. Inside my head I said, you damn skippy I want my job back! But when I opened my mouth, a loud and clear "NO!" escaped.

As I was walking away from Andre, mad at my ego for saying no, Chris Rock approached me.

"Can I give you a ride home?" he asked me.

"Sure," I said. "I'm going uptown to Dyckman."

Chris looked confused. "I thought you lived in Brooklyn?"

"I'm going to my sister's house. She stays in Dyckman."

"I'm not going all the way up there," Chris said. "I thought you were going to Brooklyn."

Since Chris decided not to drive me to Dyckman, Elaine was concerned about my safety, so she asked George Harrell—an Uptown employee not related to Andre—if he'd do the honors to make sure I got home safely. George expressed interest in doing so, and we left the party—me, Elaine, and George. Elaine lived in the vicinity, so she walked home, and I walked with George to his car and then we drove off.

I never much liked George, even when we were co-workers at Uptown Records, but I trusted him to at least get me to my destination as he'd promised. When we reached Harlem, George pulled over and put his car into park. "I'll be right back," he told me. I watched him as he ran across the street and disappeared into a rundown tenement building.

Behind the Music

Since I was born in Harlem and knew the neighborhood well, I wasn't afraid sitting there by myself. Around roughly fifteen minutes later, George was back in his car, and we continued going uptown.

As we neared Dyckman Housing Projects, I pointed to my sister's building and said, "Right there, George. Drop me off right over there." George ignored me and continued to drive pass my sister's building. "Why didn't you stop?" I asked him. He said nothing and continued driving until we reached an unsafe-looking neighborhood in the Bronx.

I wasn't all that familiar with the Bronx. I never felt safe in that rundown, neglected borough, filled with abandoned buildings. "Why did you bring me all the way up here, George?" I asked.

Finally, he spoke. "I live over there," he said.

I turned my head around to see what was over there. The only building I saw was a Housing Projects. George pulled out a brown paper bag and opened it to let me get a peek inside of it. "Lets go upstairs to my place," he said pointing to the bag to apparently entice me as if I was a crackheaded ho. I wondered what gave him that impression about me.

"I don't want to go to your house, George. I don't even like you like that. And I don't do drugs."

"What if I make you come upstairs?"

"If you touch me, you're gonna get what I got in my pocketbook!"

"And what's that?"

"Touch me and find out."

"Get out of my car!" George yelled. "I'm not taking you home! Take a cab!"

In the wee hours, in a bummy, rundown section of the Bronx, I got out of George's car, which happened to be parked right in front of a cab station. I was thankful for that. But most of all, I was thankful I had enough money to pay for the taxi ride back to my sister's place.

Bucky and I were still in contact with each other as if he hadn't done me dirty. I didn't realize it then, but apparently, I didn't love myself. If I did, Bucky would've been kicked to the curb a long time ago. That's what a woman with lots of love and respect for herself would've done.

Anyhow, I was surprised when a few weeks after running into Andre and Chris Rock at that celebrity party, Bucky informed me that Andre had terminated him.

"Why?" I asked.

Bucky said something about Andre said his contract was up and his services were no longer needed. Because of the timing, I immediately wondered if his dismissal had something to do with that made-up story about security throwing me out of Uptown's party—hmmm.

Now that Bucky was suffering the same fate as I had, he asked if I could go with him to the unemployment office because he was embarrassed to be seen there alone.

Since I had experience receiving unemployment checks and since I was still being a decent friend to Bucky, I went along for moral support and as we stood in line, I explained the process and what he could expect.

CHAPTER 20

Spring 1992

My love for the music game was still strong, and I wanted back in. I submitted my resume to Zomba (Jive) Records, the label of Britney Spears, R. Kelly, and a slew of other platinum-selling artists; not long after, I was hired by Barry Weiss, the general manager at that time. He hired me right over the phone, sight unseen.

"You sure you don't have any other positions available?" I asked.

"No. That's all we have a need for right now."

I swallowed my pride and accepted the position as the company's switchboard operator. I figured once in, I'd worm my way into another position. Although life at Zomba was no match for the good times I'd had at Uptown Records, at least I was back in the game.

I got along fairly well with my new co-workers. Everything was all good; especially the times R. Kelly popped up and made my heart go pitter-patter.

Behind the Music

"I like your outfit," I told Kelly one of those times he popped up. He had on a two-piece pajama-like outfit with a stocking cap to match. It was unique.

"Thank you," he said. He seemed bashful at first, nothing at all like the person I'd seen humping around onstage.

"It's really nice," I continued.

Then, before I knew it, Kelly had made his way closer to the switchboard station. He looked me up and down. "You're a cutie," he said.

"Thanks," I said as I carried on with the zillion-and-one phone lines, pretending as though his flattering remark didn't have my heart pitter-pattering all day long.

Regrettably, the good times at Zomba came to a screeching halt when Bucky called the office one day. When I answered the switchboard, he recognized my voice, of course. After that, he popped up nearly every day, hanging around the switchboard station, grinning in my face, acting like he and I were still ace boon coon the way we used to be during the early stages of my tenure at Uptown.

He told me he'd applied for employment at Zomba, to no avail. He even suggested that he and I start a business together. Imagine that.

"No!" I told him. "All you ever do is belittle me!"

After that, I noticed that whenever Bucky came around, he was in the ears of the employees I spent most of my time hanging around at the switchboard. Not long after Bucky appeared, that circle of co-workers who hung around the switchboard stopped being cool with me. Coincidence? I think not. Was Bucky trying to get me blackballed? I think yes.

Every day thereafter, those same co-workers harassed me about one thing or another. They were unkind to me every day, sometimes making little snide comments about my positions at Uptown Records, something I'd never discussed with any of them.

They would accuse me of doing things I didn't do, in hopes of getting me in trouble with management. One of them, a dark-skinned, strikingly thin woman who'd bragged about being DJ Grandmaster Flash's girlfriend, was extra mean to me. If I'm not mistaken, her name was Lisa Brown.

One day as I walked past Ms. Brown, she pointed at me, laughed and whispered in the ear of another co-worker as if she had a big juicy secret on me. I knew she and the other co-workers were conspiring against me. Why? I didn't have proof, but I had a big clue: Bucky.

One morning I arrived at work; I hadn't even been there a whole fifteen minutes before the harassment began. I didn't want or need that kind of drama in my peaceful life, so instead of thuggin' it out and putting up with my mean co-workers, I sat at the switchboard station and wrote a *thank-you-for-the-opportunity-but-sorry-I-quit* note to Barry Weiss and placed it in his office before he arrived that morning. Then I walked off the job without telling anyone, leaving the switchboard unattended.

I felt sort of bad about leaving in that manner, especially because Barry Weiss was always pleasant to me. And when he hired me, there really was no opening for a switchboard operator. I would come to find out he'd created an opening for me by first having the current switchboard operator train me for one day, then the next day he fired her, to her surprise, as well as mine, simply because he just didn't like her attitude toward him. But that wasn't my circus, wasn't my monkeys.

I was done with all the drama behind the music, and frankly, I was fed up with New York City, too.

August 1993

I packed up my children and just the bare minimum of what I would need or what could fit into my friend's red Jetta. I left all my other furniture behind, then I waved goodbye to New York as I set out on my fool's journey to a whole new world, a place I'd never visited before, nor did I know anyone living there.

PART III

SLEEPING WITH THE ENEMY

Rider-Waite Tarot Deck

codependency: the tie that binds

CHAPTER 21

Lucifer and I met in Georgia at Underground Atlanta, a shopping and entertainment district in the Five Points neighborhood of downtown Atlanta, the summer of 1994.

It had been nearly a year after I'd settled into a one-bedroom apartment in the city of Decatur.

This was the first time I'd lived in or seen an apartment complex with swimming pools, a lake, fitness center, tennis and racket courts, and no rats. You couldn't tell me I wasn't living large with my two walk-in closets, a dishwasher, a crystal chandelier in the dining area, and a balcony that contained a spacious closet for extra storage.

I tried to picture myself living in something like this in the City of New York. No way could I've gotten an 800-square foot apartment like this for a measly four hundred and fifteen bucks per month. No siree!

In New York City, an apartment such as this, back in the 90s, would, first of all, cost about a good one or two grand, if not more.

Today, we are talking 'bout roughly a good three or four grand per month, and the apartment will be mad tiny with beady-eyed mice running around leaving trails of little black doo-doo balls.

After my first week in Georgia, I wasted no time finding employment as a temp. Temping had always been a blessing to me whenever I was in-between jobs but still had to pay bills.

During one of my long-term assignments, I met Angela Threats. She was a temp, too. She was one of the first persons I'd met before Lucifer. We instantly clicked.

Angie had recently moved from Rhode Island to Georgia, and not only were we co-workers, we were neighbors, too. She lived roughly one mile from me.

After six months in Georgia, I was missing my sister, and I wanted to share my new beautiful life with her. She was still living in Dyckman Houses with her four children, struggling to kick a drug habit she'd acquired—so I called her and told her to join me.

She was elated, and so was I because she was more than a sister; she was my best friend. So, we both agreed a new and different scenery was what she needed to kick her habit.

My sister and her newly born youngest child joined me and my children several weeks later. She retrieved her other three children, who were left in Millie's care, upon obtaining her own apartment a few months later.

Today, my sister is still a resident of Georgia. She is drug-free. And she has recently obtained her master's degree in christian counseling.

Underground Atlanta was also the spot where many wannabe artists showcased their talents for donations. Lucifer was the lead singer of a band that included a trumpeter and a flutist, and they were one of the regulars who performed there.

The first time I heard Lucifer sing, I was blown away. Had I not seen him in person, I'd have sworn I was listening to the late Gerald Levert (the son of Eddie Levert, lead singer of The O'Jays, an R&B vocal group).

Nearly every day that summer in 1994, I'd head on down to the Underground to hear ol' boy sing and sometimes my new friend, Angie, accompanied me; she'd developed a liking for one of Lucifer's bandmates.

There was always a large crowd of onlookers as if Lucifer and his bandmates were a well-known famous act; that's how crowded it was whenever they'd perform.

And as might be expected, they received hundreds of dollars in their plastic charity collection bucket whenever they'd perform.

Although I was mesmerized by Lucifer's voice, his bad attitude turned me off. I noticed he was always angry and rude to his audience. He'd yell at them, "Back up!" and when some of the females called him fat, he'd say, "Fuck you, bitch!"

I didn't know him then, but I couldn't stand him. About five-foot-seven-inches tall, weighing in at roughly 295 pounds—give or take a little—Lucifer looked ugly to me. Not my type at all—ugh!

One day after he and his bandmates had finished performing, I walked up to the flutist, since he seemed more professional and nicer, and introduced myself. I told him I had experience in the music industry and maybe I could manage them or something.

When the flutist introduced me to the rest of the band, Lucifer was suddenly kind and charming and came on to me like a whirlwind. To my surprise, I was instantly drawn to him, too, and within two months of courting, Lucifer convinced me to move in with him into a two-story townhouse in the city of Clarkston, a small city surrounded by Atlanta, Decatur, and Stone Mountain.

Since I'd never shacked up with a man before, let alone a full-blown pathological, narcissistic, sociopath, I had no clue what I was in for. So, in next to no time, this kind-charmer turned back into that ugly, fat, angry man I'd first seen, and we'd argue nearly every day, mostly about sex.

"Sex is not the most important thing in a relationship," I'd say.

"Well, to me it is!" Lucifer would snap back.

Unfortunately, Lucifer had no clue or understanding that a woman like me needed more than a small, short penis

Sleeping with the Enemy

to ignite her fire. He just didn't seem to grasp that concept. So, the angrier he became, the more I recoiled from him.

Sex with Lucifer never felt right to my soul since day one, mainly because the first time it happened, he raped me, as far as I was concerned. Until now, I've never shared this with anyone, but I didn't want to have sex with Lucifer that night.

However, I placed myself in a certain situation with him and when things were getting too hot and steamy for him, I said, "No!" unsuccessfully. I even tried to push him off me, but he was much stronger and bigger than me. I felt like it was my fault for putting myself there; so, when he started strong-arming me, I simply gave in and just let it happen to get it over with quicker and within a peaceful manner, if you know what I mean. But deep within my soul, he violated me, and that was the beginning of the end of my five-year karmic cycle with him.

Despite that, I'm not saying Lucifer wasn't good in bed. He was great at laying down the pipe. Seemingly, it was the only other thing he could do as well as sing. In fact, he was so good at having sex, I didn't even pay much attention to the fact that he had a teeny-weeny until he brought it up, claiming that one of the mothers of his children told him his dick was little.

She ultimately left him for another man, perhaps, a big dick man. But, that's beside the point. My other core issue with Lucifer was that I didn't feel spiritually connected to him. We didn't have a soul to soul connection. And I wasn't in love with him.

So, eventually sex with Lucifer felt like a chore, an unpleasant one. In fact, it got to a point when most times, the touch of his hand on any parts of my body, including my hand, made my skin crawl, a clear indication he wasn't my Prince Charming or Twin Flame, and I certainly wasn't his Black Cinderella.

The glass slipper did not fit. It wasn't an energetic match, even though, in most cases, you will only attract what you're a vibrational match to but there are instances, such as this—I've convinced myself—when you'll attract what's needed to swiftly advance your soul to a higher level of consciousness or it could be a karmic debt of some sort—yikes.

I can just hear him now, the late Johnny Cochran, saying: "If the shoe doesn't fit, you must dip (out)!" Instead of setting myself free, I remained in this toxic relationship and, reluctantly and sporadically, I'd have sex with Lucifer, too.

"Hurry up!" I'd yell at Lucifer whenever he'd lay on top of my stiff body, sweat dripping from his face as his fat feet curled until he got a cramp in his leg. "You're taking too long! Hurry up, already!"

A little while later, Lucifer and I moved into another home, a house for rent. It was in Decatur. Before long, we were back at it: arguing virtually every day about sex.

Since we had extra rooms in the house, I decided it was high time I had my own room. Not only was I tired of sharing the same messy room, the same bed, and the same tiny closet buried with cupcakes, chocolate candy bars, and porn magazines, I'd mostly had enough of Lucifer groping on me every night as we lay in bed together—yuck.

In my own private bedroom, sometimes Lucifer would come there late at night and sit on the edge of the bed. "Can you please get in bed with me?" he'd plead. "I don't like us sleeping in different beds." After he'd leave the room unaccompanied, head bowed in sorrow, a sinister cloud always lingered behind him.

One night—I'll never forget this night—while I was lying in bed tucked underneath the covers about to get my sleep on, Lucifer was standing by the foot of my bed pouting and growling at me about something. Probably sex. Like, what else? Then suddenly, he stormed out of the bedroom and out the front door. Good riddance, I thought.

As I was rolling from my left side onto my right side, I saw something out of the corner of my eye. When did Lucifer come back? I didn't even hear him open the front door or the shuffling of shoes against the floor. I turned onto my back and saw Lucifer standing at the foot of the bed staring at me. He didn't say one word. Unease slithered down my spine. He was giving me the heebie-jeebies.

Finally, my eyes pierced through the pitch-darkness of the room. Ohmygod! Lucifer horrorstruck the bejesus out of me, and the last thing I saw before the pillow covered my face as the light in my eyes went black wasn't Lucifer, per se. It was a solid opaque-black entity, a stout silhouette shadow man who looked just like Lucifer: similar physique, similar looking lightweight waist-length jacket, except shadow man had no eyes. I didn't see any facial features, either.

I don't know how long I was out cold, but when I came to, I was suffocating. My arms were pinned down as I laid flat on my back, and as hard as I tried, I could not move or scream as if I was paralyzed. After a long couple of seconds, right before suffocating to death, I snatched the pillow off my face and gasped for air—whew!

Where did shadow man go? He was nowhere in sight. Maybe he attached himself back to Lucifer. I didn't know where he went, but what I did know was that I never wanted to see that creepy black nigga ever again.

The next day when Lucifer returned to the house, to be double sure, I asked him, "Did you come right back after you left?"

Granted, Lucifer was a habitual liar, but I knew he was telling the truth when he gave me a peculiar look and said, "No. I didn't come back." Just as I knew—way back in the day (early 70s)—my brother, Ty, was telling the truth when as young children playing hide-and-go-seek in our choo-choo train apartment, he had hidden himself in the kitchen behind the stove and before I could finish counting up to ten, my brother, in a state of sheer terror, ran out of his hiding place claiming he'd seen a tall man dressed in a black top hat and a long black trench coat appear out of nowhere.

My mother, Millie, reported Ty's sighting to Mr. Shapiro, the landlord of the building, and Mr. Shapiro told Millie that the Hat Man my brother had sighted was his dead Jewish brother.

Whatever, I'll never forget the day my brother saw a Jewish Shadow Man just as I'll never forget the day I saw a spine-chilling shadow of Lucifer. And even though I tried and tried to rationalize it by telling myself it was all a dream, the truth of the matter is I wasn't dreaming.

Apart from that scary moment, Lucifer silently and sullenly dealt with my new sleeping arrangement until the evening of January 11, 1996. He could no longer stand us sleeping in separate rooms; so, he grabbed me and forced me into his bedroom and shut the door. I swiftly managed to escape from his grip and out of his room. What he'd planned to do to me while locked in his room, I can only guess.

Anyways, seething, Lucifer stormed out of the room and into the living room where he found my son and I planted on the sofas. Lucifer stood awhile in thought, then picked up the house phone and dialed 911. "She's beating on me!" he lied to the 911 operator.

Shortly thereafter, three police officers were standing in our living room looking for bruises on Lucifer's fat body.

"I don't see anything," one of the officers said.

"Right there!" Lucifer said, pointing at his fat ashy hand. "She scratched me right there! See?"

"Look!" the officer said, a tad annoyed. "I don't see any scratch marks. Maybe you should go for a walk until you calm down."

A walk to calm down? That was the wrong advice to give a person with a vindictive personality disorder. Revenge is what was on Lucifer's mind, not a walk to calm himself down. Lucifer had a plan and it was to have them arrest me just as they had arrested him two months prior, November 10, 1995.

November 10, 1995

As usual, Lucifer was angry. It bothered him greatly to see me and my son hanging out in my son's bedroom enjoying *Martin* when I could be having sex with him. Comedian Martin Lawrence and the cast in the sitcom had my son and I rolling in laughter.

Naturally, Lucifer had to find a way to turn my smile into a frown; so, he shut off all the power. The whole house went black. Since Lucifer had done this once before, it didn't take me as long as the first time to figure out he'd unscrewed the fuse in the fuse box, so I simply found my way through the pitch-black house to the fuse box and screwed the fuse back in its socket, then continued to watch *Martin*.

Well, that didn't sit too well with Lucifer, and he grew angrier. His anger led him to grab my pocketbook. While rummaging through my purse, he yelled, "Give me your key to the house. I want you out!"

"Give me my pocketbook," I yelled back. I followed Lucifer into his bedroom.

"Give me the key and get out!"

I tried to grab my purse from Lucifer's hands, but he wrestled me onto his bed and sat his fat ass on top of my chest. Once he took the house key out of my bag, he slashed me straight across my face with it, directly underneath my right eye. If I didn't know any better, I'd swear he was trying to remove my eye from its socket just as he had removed the fuse from its socket.

When my son, who was 13 at the time, heard all the commotion and saw Lucifer manhandling me, as blood trickled down my face, he immediately dialed 911 as he should've. By the time the cops had arrived, Lucifer had covered up all the blood on his bed while I rushed to the bathroom and stood in front of the mirror thinking about how I went from simply watching TV to this?

As I tried to stop the blood from dripping down my face with a white towel, I heard one of the officers yell out, "Come out, ma'am! We need to see you."

I pressed the towel against the wound and walked into the living room.

"Move the towel away from your face, ma'am," one of the officers said. When I did as I was instructed, blood began oozing out of the slit on my face. The two officers' eyes grew wide and they swiftly drew their guns and pointed directly at Lucifer as if they were prepared to blast him to smithereens; then they ordered him to put down the weapon he'd moments ago used on me.

Meanwhile, I silently prayed they weren't officers with the same mindset as the Governor of Maine (Paul LePage) who believed Blacks and Hispanics were the enemy, and therefore, "You shoot at the enemy," LePage claimed. Thank goodness they weren't race soldiers; they were real cops—whew!

The medics came to examine my bruised face, and of course, Lucifer was straightaway handcuffed and taken to jail. He spent a few hours incarcerated before bailing out, and then, at the end of it all, he was sentenced to an anger management class.

Rewind back to January 11, 1996

Instead of feeling remorseful for physically abusing me on November 10, 1995, Lucifer had no conscience at all. The only thing he cared about was retaliation. He wanted me to know what it felt like in jail, too. As far as he was concerned, it was all my fault my son had enough sense to call the police on him when he drew blood from my face.

Had I only given him sex or let him rape me again, he wouldn't have had any reason to slash my face. So, yeah, I was to blame; it was all my doing.

Unfortunately, on the evening of January 11, 1996, the officers didn't understand Lucifer's plan. They didn't know that the person calling them had a Jussie Smollett personality disorder; you know the kind: when you call the police, faking like someone attacked you. They didn't know that his call to them was simply a 'payback' call, not a 'walk to calm down' call. No, no, no! The officers had it all wrong!

"If I have to leave," Lucifer told the officers, "I'm taking everything with me." Full of rage, Lucifer unplugged my desktop computer, the one he'd recently bought me, the one I was having a love affair with. He picked it up and headed toward the front door.

"Put my computer down!" I yelled at Lucifer as I tried to grab it out of his hands. He pushed me away, then I pushed him right back.

"Okay. That's enough!" one of the officers said. "Since you want to call us and waste our time with this foolishness, you're both under arrest. Now, put your hands behind your back."

One of the officers placed my children in the back of his patrol car and took them to my sister's house. The other two officers cuffed me and Lucifer, then placed us in the back of their patrol car.

While in route to the county jail, I slid my bony wrists out of my cuffs, while Lucifer not only complained to the officers that his cuffs were too tight on his fat wrists, he also begged them to take us back home.

I turned to Lucifer and said, "Are you happy now?" Then I rolled my eyes at him before turning away in disgust.

We spent a few hours in separate holding cells before we were bailed out. The case was later dismissed.

Strike one.

CHAPTER 22

Not surprisingly my relationship with Lucifer didn't improve. In fact, it had me severely stressed out all day, every day. I became increasingly depressed, too. I found myself getting sick on a regular basis.

Lucifer had a serious back problem. His back ached so badly, sometimes we'd have to rush to the hospital so that he could get a shot in his ass to make him feel better. In time, my back ached, too, an issue I'd never had prior to meeting Lucifer.

My hair was falling out, too, looking mad dry and scrappy. My weight was spiraling down, down, down. I was disappearing into thin air. I must've weighed around 96 pounds, maybe less. Whatever the amount, I was excessively scrawny, and it felt like I was carrying ten heavy rods on my back everywhere I went. I looked and felt totally drained.

To make matters worse, Lucifer had the audacity to tell me, "I'm ashamed of you around my friends."

"You're ashamed of me?" I retorted. "I need to be ashamed of you...you big, fat, ugly, broke-ass whale!"

I couldn't take Lucifer and this way of living any longer, always walking on eggshells, looking over my shoulders. I had to constantly watch my back because Lucifer was relentlessly scheming, looking for different ways to consciously hold me down, believing that was the only way to keep me around.

Sadly, Lucifer didn't realize that the way to my heart was simply being nice, trustworthy, and respectful...or maybe he did know.

"I don't want to be alone. I'm in this for the long haul, but I know you're going to leave me...." he'd say to me from time to time as if he clearly understood he wasn't good to me but had no control over his behavior. Although he may have wanted me as his life partner, he knew he was out of my league; he knew my worth and value more than I did, regrettably.

So, when I was sad, it made Lucifer glad. When I was glad, it made Lucifer mad. Life with Lucifer had turned me into someone I absolutely didn't know or like. What happened to that energized, happy person who was enjoying her new life in the south before Lucifer appeared? I wanted her back. Something had to give. I wanted my power back, too; the power I'd allowed Lucifer to slowly but surely drain out of me.

I did not trust him at all and felt unsafe in his presence. By this time, it was obvious to me that he was trying to destroy my life or kill me, but for some peculiar reason, as if I was under a spell of some sort…a karmic debt, possibly, I continued to sleep with the enemy, giving him chance after chance after chance to ruin my life…until February 23, 1997.

February 23, 1997

Although Lucifer had drained out virtually all my oomph, I had a drop or two left to finally muster up the strength to leave him…again. This was going to be my second time around. The first time was January 12, 1996, the day after strike one (my first arrest). Lucifer tried to make it difficult for me to leave then. This time, I wanted to leave in peace, but with him around that was out of the question; so, I waited until he went to work the evening of February 23rd before calling an associate to swing by with his moving truck. I even made it my business to be extra nice to Lucifer that morning.

I sensed that Lucifer had sensed that I had been making plans to leave him. Psychos are usually pretty good at reading their victims like a book and knowing their every move. So, I wasn't too surprised when he told me he'd noticed that my dishware kept vanishing from the cubbyhole, dishware I'd been stashing, little by little, into my new apartment in the city of Atlanta, the place I'd secretly acquired weeks before.

On more than one occasion, Lucifer would leave the house to supposedly report to his night job and then about an hour or two later, he'd slink back into the house, claiming he'd decided not to go to work that day.

Well, after he'd done that more than twice, I quickly caught on to what he was really doing. He was trying to catch me moving out on him. So, I knew a little nooky in the morning would convince this sex addict all was good between us and he'd feel secure enough to go to work and stay his butt there until I was long gone. And just as I'd planned, the sex scheme worked.

I didn't see Lucifer until the next day when I had this brilliant idea to go shopping in his neck of the woods, although it did occur to me that maybe I'd see him.

I kept my son out of school that day because I knew his school would be the first place Lucifer would look for me. He knew I drove my son to and from school every day. So, with my son in the passenger's seat, I drove to Decatur, where I was used to shopping. As I pulled up into Belvedere Shopping Plaza on Columbia Drive, which was literally right around the corner from Lucifer's house, there he was on a pay phone.

He instantly spotted my 1984 tan colored Camaro at the same time I spotted him. Not wanting a confrontation, I quickly made a U-turn up out of that plaza. Lucifer dropped the phone and leaped into his car. The chase was on and popping!

Like a deranged madman, he chased me, ignoring every red light. I made a right turn on to Memorial Drive, and Lucifer was right on my tail, barely missing banging into other vehicles. I was terrified; I could feel his angry energy piercing through my soul. So, I silently prayed his car would spin out of control as I drove as fast and as safely as possible, with trembling legs, to the nearest police station.

When I arrived at the police station, there wasn't one officer in sight. They were never around when I needed them. Nevertheless, I jumped out of my car and ran to the first door I saw. It was locked.

"Help!" I yelled while banging on the door. Finally, two young, black male officers appeared. As soon as Lucifer saw them, he jumped out of his car.

"She's got a warrant!" he yelled before I could get one word out.

"Ma'am, we first have to check to see if you have a warrant," one of the officers said.

Once they verified there was actually a warrant out for my arrest—the one Lucifer had obviously taken out when he came home from work and realized I'd packed up all of my furniture and moved out—I was told to put my hands behind my back and then once again I was cuffed right in front of my son.

I swear, I truly hated for my son to see me like that, let alone once, but now a second time. My daughter, now eighteen, had returned to New York to live with Millie after my first strike, so she missed this episode. What bothered me the most, however, was the fact that I was going to jail for the second frickin' time.

Until Lucifer had entered my life, no one could have ever convinced me that I'd end up in jail. I didn't even see it coming. I was so naïve and too trusting of people. I thought everyone was like me. Unfortunately, when you're green, you don't know it until you're no longer green or naïve. It's just like being brainwashed. When you're brainwashed, quite naturally you don't know you're brainwashed. You really believed, during the 'separate but equal' Jim Crow era, the water in the fountains labeled *'White Only'* tasted better than the water in the fountains labeled *'Colored Only.'*

But, once you're no longer brainwashed, it is then and only then that you can clearly see that everything you thought you knew, you thought was true, was all an illusion or your perception or simply a big juicy fib.

Nonetheless, as the officers took me inside the precinct with my son tagging along, carrying my pocketbook, the wide grin on Lucifer's face said it all: mission accomplished.

I was placed inside a cell with vertical bars. My son, fortunately, was allowed to talk to me through the bars until my sister came and got him and my car.

Later that day I was transported to Dekalb County Jail, where I met with the detective assigned to my case.

"Why was I arrested?" I asked the young black detective.

"He said you were homeless and out of the kindness of his heart, he offered you a place to live, and this is the thanks he got: you robbed him."

"Whaaaaaaat?" I shrieked. "He said I was homeless and what?"

"Here," the detective said as he shoved a pad and pen at me. "Write down what happened."

I wrote that Lucifer had rummaged through my personal files and stole my son's social security number. By the time my intuition told me to open the trunk of Lucifer's car, I was sitting in front of Towers High School, where I'd just dropped off my son. Because my car's gas tank was empty, I'd taken the key to Lucifer's car off the nightstand while he was asleep.

"Look underneath the spare tire," my intuition told me. I had no clue what I was looking for but when I saw it, I couldn't believe my eyes when I saw Lucifer's tax return with my son's name on it and eight hundred dollars in cash that was left from the nearly seven thousand that Lucifer had received from the Internal Revenue Service. Of course, I pocketed the money and Lucifer's tax return, but that was the straw that broke the camel's back and sent me packing.

I knew I had to get away from Lucifer. Our relationship wasn't getting better. It was getting worse. I knew it was never going to get better because I was sleeping with a cotton pickin' devil—a black [d]evil.

I knew that if I didn't leave this demon alone, there would be a strike three, if not death. If death, Lucifer would've cleverly convinced law enforcement that I'd killed myself or that I'd had an accident.

I was initially charged with theft by taken, but somewhere along the line, it was changed to shoplifting. Anyways, after reading my handwritten statement, the detective assigned to my case promised to get me out. And true to his word, within seventy-two hours, I was released on my own recognizance.

Two months later, Lucifer and I appeared in front of a judge. After we said our piece (Lucifer and I), the case was dismissed but not before the judge scolded Lucifer and threatened to make him pay a fine for perjury and for playing games with the judicial system.

Strike two.

CHAPTER 23

Instead of suing Lucifer for malicious prosecution, I was a tad lonely and still didn't know my true value and worth. I didn't know what loving myself meant so why did I expect Lucifer to know how to properly love me when we teach others how to treat us?

So, by letting him back into my life straight after the dismissal of the case, I was teaching Lucifer that he had my permission to continue to treat me like trash, except this time, we continued to live in separate dwellings: my choice.

I was at least learning that I'd have more control over my own life if we didn't live together…but, did I really grasp the lesson this karmic relationship was trying to teach me? And, could I pass the final exam?

Lucifer, however, wasn't accustomed to living alone or being alone for too long. That was his greatest fear: being alone. Thus, he'd developed a pattern of overlapping—jumping into a new relationship before completely ending an old one.

So, it was during this time, while we'd been living apart for well over two years, Lucifer had ample freedom to know other women, which led to the day when I became one of them. You know the kind: a ratchet dimwitted fool working from the lower aspects within oneself, the kind you see on those ratchet reality shows such as the *Fake*...I mean, *Real Housewives of Atlanta* and *Love and Hip Hop*.

It happened on a balmy summer evening, August 2, 1999. I was lounging on Lucifer's living room sofa watching the six o'clock news while guzzling down a home-cooked plate of soul food. Suddenly, she marched directly in front of me with a stormy look upon her face, hands propped on her hips. "Get out, heifer!" she shouted at me.

She was one of the other women Lucifer got to know while he and I were living in separate dwellings. The first time I became aware of her existence was on a sunny afternoon in 1998. Lucifer and I had plans to go jogging...or was it the time we were going to check out a free concert in the park?

Since Lucifer had no car during this time, I picked him up at his house. As I was pulling into his driveway, I noticed her standing near the porch as small children played nearby. She watched as Lucifer got into my car on the passenger's side. As I was backing up out of the driveway, I inquired about her.

"She's my cousin's wife," Lucifer told me.

"Where's your cousin?"

Sleeping with the Enemy

"He's out looking for a house for them."

"Oh."

According to Lucifer, they'd recently moved to Georgia, and needed a temporary place to live while searching for their own house.

Although Lucifer had been a pathological liar throughout the few years I'd known him, I had no reason not to believe that story.

For as long as I'd known Lucifer, his home had always been a revolving door for all his family members, friends, and his friends' friends. Everybody was welcomed, including strangers. So, seeing her there wasn't unusual, but it was surprising to me because up until then, Lucifer had never mentioned her and his cousin to me as he'd did all of his other housemates and guests, including his best friend, Sean.

Lucifer knew I wasn't the jealous type. I'd never had a problem with Lucifer having female friends, and he'd introduced me to many of them. So, months after I'd moved out, Lucifer asked me if I'd be okay with Sean and her children moving in. Of course, I had no problem with that. She'd been Lucifer's friend long before I entered the picture, so, as far as I was concerned, a friend of his was a friend of mine.

Sean was tall, slim, and light-skinned...really, really light like Faith Evans (The Notorious B.I.G. aka Biggie Smalls' wife). She was drop-dead gorgeous, and she and I became chummy-chummy because, according to Lucifer, she'd expressed to him that I was the only girlfriend he had, who she'd met, who didn't have a problem with her hanging around. Since I didn't have an issue with her. She was always a guest in our home when Lucifer and I lived together; so, when she became his roomie, sometimes she and her children joined Lucifer and I on local trips, and she was always a pleasure to have around.

Thus, when I pulled up in the driveway and saw this woman and children that Lucifer had never mentioned to me, standing there in the front yard, I was flabbergasted. But when she said nothing to Lucifer when he got into my car, I was convinced she was Lucifer's cousin's wife, and even when I'd stopped by the house to pick up Lucifer a few more times, she never said anything to Lucifer or me as she watched us drive away.

I even stopped by once late in the evening, after eleven o'clock. When Lucifer opened his front door, I noticed it was dark inside, and she was standing behind him. That's when I became suspicious. Why was Lucifer's cousin's wife at the door with my man in her nightgown, stretching her neck to see who was there for him? Shouldn't she be in bed with her husband at this time of night? Why hadn't Lucifer introduced us by now? And where was Lucifer's cousin? I'd still not met him, either; so, when Lucifer left the house and got in my car, I inquired again about her husband's whereabouts as we drove off to go visit my sister.

Of course, Lucifer fed me more lies, so I left it alone. I'm sure he was feeding her a bunch of mendacities about me, too. But whatever he told her about me, up until this point, she knew I was more than a friend. I'm certain of that.

One evening during the spring of 1998, my son and I popped up at the Underground where Lucifer and his band were performing. When Lucifer spotted me, I noticed the panicky look carved on his face.

After the show was over, Lucifer called me over to him. While we were talking, Lucifer's cousin's wife walked up on us and before she could get a complete sentence out of her mouth, Lucifer yelled at her, "Get the fuck away from us, bitch!"

Bewildered, I turned to Lucifer and asked, "Why are you talking to her like that?" I didn't recognize her as the woman living in Lucifer's house, Lucifer's cousin's wife, because at this point, I'd never gotten a clear, good detailed look at her. She tried to say something again, and as before, Lucifer yelled, "Get the fuck away, bitch! Get out of here, stupid bitch!"

I turned to her and asked, "Who are you?"

Lucifer was determined to not let her speak, and so once again he yelled, "Get away from us, bitch! Then, he grabbed my hand and said to me, "Come on, Vanessa, take a walk with me. Let's move away from that stupid bitch."

I grabbed my hand back from Lucifer's hand and said, "No! You walk away. I want to hear what she got to say." When Lucifer walked away, I asked her once again, "Who are you? Is Lucifer your man or something?"

"Yes," she replied. "We've been living together for three months now. He didn't tell you about me?"

"No, he didn't. Did y'all have sex?" I asked.

"Yea."

"Did he use a condom?"

"No."

She tried to ask me a question, but I walked away from her to find Lucifer. She followed me. I found Lucifer helping his bandmates pack up their equipment. "She said she's your girlfriend," I told Lucifer. "She said y'all had sex and you didn't use a condom."

"She's lying, Baby!" Lucifer cried out.

"Baby?" she yelled at Lucifer. "Did you call her baby?"

She popped Lucifer upside his head and then they got to squabbling right in front of a crowd of onlookers. Lucifer's bandmates tried to break up the fight while my son, who was sitting off to the side, cried out to me. "Mommy! Get away from them! They are embarrassing!"

Since I was standing there dumbfounded, I took my son's advice and quickly walked away from those two clowns and sat next to my son. We watched the dog and cat fight for a few more moments, then we got up and left.

Weeks went by since that day, and Lucifer was still denying their relationship, even though they were still living together. I wanted a change of pace so by summertime, I sold some of my furniture, gave some away to my sister and others, and, like a fool, I left my car in Lucifer's care, then went to New York and lived out there with my mother and children.

New York was good for me during that time. I even put some meat on my bones and became that happy, cute, energized person again. And all the while I was in New York, Lucifer and I spoke via phone often.

During the summer of 1999, after spending a whole year in New York, I was missing Georgia and was ready to return there. But I no longer had my own place to live, so I moved back to Georgia anyways and stayed with my sister for a few weeks.

Lucifer visited me at my sister's nearly every single morning, bright and early, as if he couldn't wait to see me each day. Then, my sister had a little situation of her own, and so that left me living in a hotel for a week, paid for by one of my kindhearted male associates, the same one who used his moving truck to move me out of Lucifer's house.

After spending a week at the hotel, I asked Lucifer if I could stay at his house, and he gladly welcomed me back home. He even gave me the key to the house. There was one slight problem: Lucifer's fake cousin's wife and her three small children were still living there, too.

She was housed in the room I used to sleep in, and her children were occupying my son's old room. I needed a room to myself, so Lucifer made her move her children and all their belongings out of my son's old room and into the bedroom she was in.

The first few nights I was there, Lucifer didn't sleep in the room he used to sleep in when we lived together because one of his friends was occupying that room, so Lucifer slept on the sofa in the living room, even though he had been sharing a room with her before I arrived. But he didn't want me to know that. He was still trying to pretend they weren't a couple and she was just staying there until she found her own place. I knew better, though. That dog and cat fight at Underground Atlanta told it all.

Besides, I was seeing another guy at that point, nothing exclusive, though. So, some nights, Lucifer crept into my bedroom, my son's old room, and yes, I'd let him hit it. Not because I was horny for his affection, but mainly because I was hoping she'd catch him in the act. Yes, I was being a petty-betty, but I was also, apparently, still under a karmic spell. However, I could instinctively feel this evil, karmic cycle coming to a close.

In the meantime, the first time I got up in the wee hours and didn't see Lucifer sleeping on the couch in the living room, I knew he was sleeping in her room, in bed with her and her children.

When I questioned him about it, just for the sake of it, of course, he fed me some crazy, dumb lie. Lucifer didn't know how to tell the truth if his life depended on it. But at this stage of our situationship, I was very well aware our roles had changed—hers and mine.

She was now his main squeeze, whether Lucifer admitted it to me or not, and by the evening of August 2, 1999, she'd found out I was more than just an ex, temporary houseguest, or whatever lie Lucifer told her about me.

Monday, August 2, 1999

Like so many of us low vibrational women are known for doing, she accused me of betraying her when she'd found out Lucifer and I had had sex in his house, right up under her nose.

She found out because I told her so when one day, while Lucifer and his bandmates were out of town for the weekend, she asked me, "What's really going on between you and Lucifer?"

"Duh!" I said. "You know what's going on."

"Are y'all having sex?"

"Duh!"

Even though she and I had never bonded or built any type of friendship, nor did we have any type of agreement—verbal or written—to be faithful and true to one another, she blamed me for Lucifer's infidelity as if she didn't remember that he was still kicking it with me when he started kicking it with her. And if she wasn't for sure then, which she was, she most definitely got her confirmation when she fought with him over me at the Underground.

So as far as I was concerned, I didn't owe her any respect the same way she didn't pay me any. The only person in this third-party situationship I needed to respect was myself. But at this stage of my fool's journey, I still didn't know what self-respect and self-love looked like, and so I was sadly failing my spiritual lesson and test on self-love—before truth set me free.

Instead of standing up to me the moment I'd informed her Lucifer and I were more than friends (frenemies with benefits), she waited for him to return from his weekend gig and as soon as he walked through the front door, she got big and bad: "What the fuck is going on in here?" she yelled at Lucifer. Then she stood directly in front of me, "How could you do this to me? Get out, heifer!"

"This is not your house, sweetie," I calmly replied. "You get out."

"You gettin' the fuck out this house, bitch. He's my man now!"

"I can't tell," I said while I continued to coolly chow down on my yams and mac and cheese while shooing her away; she was blocking my view of the six o'clock news.

Since I was, for the most part, ignoring her, she approached Lucifer in their bedroom. I heard some yelling and a little scuffling going on in there, and then I heard her go into my bedroom.

To get my attention and to put the blame and focus back on me, she got one of my bags filled with my personal belongings and then she proceeded to toss out all the items in my bag, one by one, out of the bedroom and onto the floor in the hallway.

"You gettin' the fuck out of this house, bitch," she yelled a couple more times as she continued to throw my things on the floor in the hallway. Then I heard my new sweet-smelling expensive bottle of perfume crash into tiny pieces as it hit the floor.

I waited a few moments for Lucifer to intercede; after all, she was supposed to be his problem, not mine. So quite naturally I expected him to man up and rectify his issue. But he was mad at me for telling her his secret which he assumed was "our" little secret. He presumed that I was now his secret lover, and we were in cahoots to deceive her. Unfortunately, telling her backed fired on me, as I knew it would, and they both ended up blaming me—for different reasons—and ganging up on me.

So instead of Lucifer calming her down, he acted as though he knew neither one of us, and to further remove himself from the situation that was clearly getting way out of hand, he picked up the cordless phone, stepped over my belongings on the floor in the hallway and bolted out the front door.

Now, what was I supposed to do with his problem that had turned into my problem? Of course, my God or Higher-Self told me to pack up my belongings and leave, never to return.

Ignoring my Higher-Self, as you might expect from someone vibrating at a low frequency, I sat my plate of food on the coffee table, then straightened out my ratchet dimwitted fool crown. I had to make sure that bad boy was propped up just right on my head before I showed this aggravating hussy a thing or two about messing with me.

"I'm sick of you, you stupid ass crack ho," I said as my index finger found its way to her forehead to poke at it while I gave her a piece of my mind. Then the fight was on and cracking. By the time Lucifer reappeared, it was too late; she was losing a lot of blood.

"Call an ambulance!" Lucifer yelled at her as he stood between both of us but keeping his eyes mainly on me, afraid I would do more damage.

By this time, I was hardly thinking about her. I had clearly done enough damage to destroy both our lives; so, the only thing on my mind was getting the heck out of Dodge before the police came to throw me in jail.

For a moment, Lucifer averted his eyes from me, and I grabbed my pocketbook that contained nearly two hundred bucks. I almost lost my footing on the bloody, slippery floor before darting out the front door. As for my belongings she'd thrown on the floor, I didn't have time to worry about that right then.

My car was parked in front of the house, but it was inoperable. It had been that way ever since I'd returned to Georgia from New York, and I had a strong suspicion of who caused it to become unworkable.

Since I had no transportation, I walked down the driveway while stashing the small deadly weapon in my pocket, my ratchet dimwitted fool crown still propped up nice. I had represented well for all the ratchet dimwitted fools around the globe fighting each other over some worthless entity.

"Now, what?" I asked my Higher-Self.

"Duh! Do the crime, do the time, that's what. You sure showed her!"

As I walked down the driveway, considering my next move, Lucifer ran up behind me. "You gotta leave! Get away from—" Before he could finish his sentence, there she was, a strikingly, skinny young woman, much younger than me and Lucifer, 'round my height, running down the driveway like a possessed bride of Chucky, yelling: "Get away from him! He's my man!"

Her grave injury must've slipped her mind when she saw Lucifer standing close to me, not knowing what he was saying. When she reached us, she began swinging her arms like an out-of-control octopus. Instead of grabbing her, Lucifer grabbed me and wrapped his fat arms around the upper part of my body as if I was the "out-of-control" cephalopod. He squeezed my arms to my sides as if I was the one who needed taming. Now I was pissed.

"Get off me!" I yelled, trying to wiggle from his grip. His hold tightened, immobilizing me. I could barely breathe.

"Get back in the house," Lucifer yelled at her. "Call the ambulance!"

She paid Lucifer no mind and tried to get at me over his big fat body. Please call an ambulance, I said to myself. I didn't want her to lose too much blood and then pass out and die. That was never my intention.

While trying to get at me, she pushed Lucifer, which in turn gave him the perfect opportunity to flip me on my back onto the sprinkled with dirt pavement while acting like it was her weak push that caused him to toss me down; I knew better, though.

While sprawled out on my back, Lucifer sat his fat ass on top of me, pinning my arms down. I twisted under his heavy body, bronco-riding and squashing me at the same time, while she was still trying to swing at me over him. A few of her baby punches landed on Lucifer's head. I chuckled to myself at how pathetic we must've looked to the neighbors.

"Call the ambulance!" Lucifer yelled again, ducking her soft baby blows. Finally, she went back to the house. Finally, Lucifer lifted his fat ass off me and left me lying on the pavement. I hastened to my feet, brushed the dirt off my clothes and out of my afro.

It was now or never. I had to get away from that house before the neighbors called the police. So to save time, I waltzed across the grass. As I passed Lucifer, I heard him talking on the cordless phone. "She's wearing a brown shirt and gray shorts."

I walked faster, trying to figure out which way the police would be coming so I could go in the opposite direction. Then I took the weapon out of my pocket, a little Swiss Army pocketknife, and threw it in the bushes nearby. I could sense I was about to have a head-on clash with the police car, so I pivoted on my heels about to take off the other way when the police pulled up beside me.

"Are you the one who got stabbed?" asked a female officer when she noticed blood on my hands and clothes. "Who did this to you? Are you hurt?" Without waiting for my response, she said, "Get in."

I got in the backseat and she drove me back to the scene. Still under the impression I was the injured party, she let me out of the patrol car to freely roam around. For a quick second, I considered running from the scene, but I knew Lucifer would rat me out, so I stayed put and waited for her to realize I was the offender.

She walked up the driveway, to the porch, where Lucifer was sitting. He was pretending like he had empathy and a conscience while fake consoling the injured party. He acted as if he had absolutely nothing to do with setting the scene for what had transpired.

As soon as Lucifer got through convincing the female officer that I was the villain, she zoomed down the driveway and approached me with a brand-new attitude. She grabbed one of my wrists, twisted it behind my back, and then threw me up against the car.

"Put your other hand behind your back," she barked. I halfheartedly did it. She helped me out and cuffed my wrists. "Spread your legs!" She frisked me and searched through my pocketbook. "Where's the knife?"

"I don't know. I dropped it."

"Where?"

"I don't know."

After she'd finished reading me my rights, I was placed in the back of her police car. I felt so dumb sitting there, my ratchet dimwitted fool crown now slanted to the side.

After the medics had placed my antagonist into the ambulance, I looked over at Lucifer. When I saw his fat ass standing on the porch acting like a superhero—there to save the day in the nick of time—I knew at that very moment this was it: the final episode of *Sleeping with the Enemy*.

Strike three.

PART IV
STATE PROPERTY

Rider-Waite Tarot Deck

change and transition

CHAPTER 24

The thick cellblock doors in pod 300 are coated orange, like my ugly jail costume, and the upper portion of the doors are an impenetrable window with no blinds or curtains. Anyone can look inside your cell and see all your business.

A switch in the control booth locks and unlocks each cell door, and when cell door 301 clangs shut behind me, the jarring sound startles me. Before I settle in, I stand near the door and give the tiny austere cell a quick scan.

The first thing I notice is a small metal sink with an attached toilet right near the door and hanging right above the sink is a small plastic, shatterproof, blurry mirror. It's so murky, I can barely see my face in it. A few inches forward, against the opposite side of the room, is a two-sided cabinet: one side is for my belongings and the other side is for the other inmate.

Next to the cabinet, is a small metal desk and chair, and at the back of the cell is a long, narrow, horizontal solid glass posing as a window. And straight across from the desk and cabinet, pushed up against the wall, is a metal, twin-size kid's bunk bed. The so-called mattress on the top cot is thin and disgustingly dirty—yuck.

Lying on the bottom bunk is that crazy girl Miss Half-Pint warned me about. Her name is Jeannette Sewell. She looks to be a tad rough around the edges; however, nothing like the burly dyke I imagined. Thank goodness! She's rather pretty. I wonder how tall she is. I guess around five-feet-nine-inches tall, weighing in at about 200 pounds. While I size her up, she does likewise.

Then she warns me: "You lucky I like you."

"Why?" I ask.

"Because I don't usually like nobody they put in here. I threw all 'dem stank smelly bitches out. If yo' ass stink, you gots to go 'cause I don't wanna be in here smelling stank ass and pus—" She stops mid-sentence to tell me I look cold. "Here. Put this on," she says before carrying on with her last sentence. "I like you, though. You're cute. You got big pretty eyes, and you don't stink; so, you can stay."

"Thanks for the t-shirt."

As I quickly put on the white, holey t-shirt, I wonder if I'll need to worry about homegirl flipping out on me. I sure hope not because I do not feel like fighting—ever again! Fighting, after all, is the reason I'm here. Plus, the last thing I'm in need of is another charge or a beat down; and by the size of Jeannette, I'm pretty sure—no, I'm positive—my five-foot-two-inch pocket-size frame will end up with the latter.

Week one

The first couple of days, I notice Jeannette sleeps a lot. She doesn't venture out of cell 301 much. So, without her by my side, I don't go out much, either. The only time Jeannette leaves cell 301 is chow time. She looks forward to those meals—three times a day.

Although I've made up my mind to never eat that nasty-looking jail food, I follow Jeannette out into the day room to get a tray of food. My sole purpose is to give my food to her. She seems to love the food. I can't understand why, though. I imagine the food tastes as nasty as it looks.

"Ugh! What is that?" I ask Jeannette as I watch her gobble every morsel on her tray.

"Shit on a Shingle," she says. "You still not gonna eat yo' food?"

"Nope," I reply. "Looks like a pile of doo-doo. You want it?"

"Hell, yeah!"

Jeannette reaches across the metal picnic table, grabs my brown plastic food tray, and wolfs down every bit of that creamy brownish gook she calls Shit on a Shingle.

I frown and wonder, how can she? I'd rather starve to death before I eat that nasty rubbish.

Before Truth Set Me Free

By the end of the first week, I'm starvin' like Marvin. Jeannette reaches across the table for my brown tray, which has become routine. I block her hands this time. "Nah, Jeannette, you can't have my food today," I tell her. I pull my tray toward me and look down at it. Yuck! What is this? Mac and Shit?

Who cares? When you're hungry you're liable to eat anything. I'm mad hungry, so I dig in and gobble up every drop of that Mac and Crap, and then I lick my fingers and finish it off with a styrofoam cup of red Kool-Aid. Ah! So refreshing!

CHAPTER 25

Week two

I still don't venture out of my cell much without Jeannette by my side. I don't like the way some of the manly looking inmates stare at me—like a juicy piece of top loin steak.

Fear must be written all over my face because Jeannette tells me, "Don't be scared, Vanessa. I got yo' back. Anybody fuck 'wit you, I'mma fuck 'em up!"

It's nice to know my back is covered, but I pray Jeannette doesn't have beef with anyone during my time here because I can't promise her I'll have her back, too. I don't want any more drama added to my life. All I want is for someone to hurry up and bail me out of this hell hole while I'm still in one solid piece—no stab wounds, no bite marks, no scratches, no nothing.

When commissary day rolls around, I share the money on my books with Jeannette—the cash I had inside my pocketbook the day I was arrested. I tell her to order ten dollars' worth of stuff.

Since she's been here, she's not been able to buy goodies from commissary because she has no money on her books, and no one comes to visit her. Because she's so appreciative, every week I allow Jeannette to order ten dollars' worth of whatever she wants.

Jeannette informs me she's a diagnosed schizophrenic. I have no clue what that means; never heard that word a day in my life. In spite of that, I don't even ask Jeannette to explain it. I just assume it's nothing I need to concern myself with even though she's on loads of medication, and at times she seems paranoid. She believes our pod is planted with spies who are out to get her, and sometimes I think she believes I'm one of the spies. At other times, she believes our cell has been invaded by creepy crawlers.

"Right there, Vanessa! You don't see 'em?"

"Nope. Where they at?"

"Right there on the floor."

"What do they look like, Jeannette?"

"Little black bugs, Vanessa. You still don't see 'em?" Jeannette then squirms, screams, and hops all around me, desperately trying to avoid stepping on the invisible black bugs.

"Girl, you are straight bugging!" I tell her, no pun intended. "Ain't no bugs on the floor."

When Jeannette isn't sleeping her time away, she and I chop it up and giggle and share stories about the life we had in the so-called free world. We even discuss the events that brought us here, and I find out, just like me, she's here because of a violent crime.

"Why did you stab them?" I ask Jeannette.

"I don't know," she replies. "We were all sitting on my sofa smoking crack, and then I got up and went to the kitchen and grabbed the butcher knife and came back into the living room and just started stabbing them for no reason."

"What did they do while you were stabbing them?"

"Dem geek monsters ran out of my house."

"Did you kill them?"

"I don't know what happened to 'em."

"So how did you end up here, then?"

"What happened was my daughter jumped on my back while I was stabbing them. She was trying to stop me and ended up cutting her hand on the knife. It wasn't even that serious. All she had was a tiny cut inside her hand."

"Where's your daughter now?"

"The state took her and charged me with aggravated battery and cruelty to children."

"How much time are they giving you?"

"Ten years. I gotta serve one year in prison, though, and the rest on probation."

Jeannette also tells me about a time when she knocked on her next-door neighbor's door.

"So, what happened?" I ask.

"When he opened the door, I just started stabbing him with a screwdriver."

"Ohmygod! Why did you do that?"

"I don't know." She giggles. "He was such a nice old man, too."

By this time, it's finally dawning on me that schizophrenia is some sort of mental disorder that distorts the way a person thinks. In most cases, as in Jeannette's case, I later learn, the person thinks someone is plotting against them.

Ah ha! No wonder Jeannette's the only inmate in our pod not allowed to have a razor. Too late! I already gave her one, and I'm not about to ask for it back, especially when I can see how happy she is to finally be able to shave her hairy armpits and hairy cooty-cat.

I silently pray, nonetheless, she doesn't have one of her episodes and uses the razor on me for no reason at all.

CHAPTER 26

Week three

I finally hang out in the dayroom without Jeannette by my side. I make friends with some of the other inmates. I find out some of them are from New York, and so I sit and chat with them about life in the Big Apple.

Toi Cordy is from New York, too. Although she's ten years younger than I, she's drawn to me like a magnet, and so we become close buddies. One thing I notice about her, though, she's a trouble starter. She seems to get a big kick out of starting arguments or talking trash to certain inmates. Not really my thing, but at times it's sort of entertaining and comical.

We laugh when she tells me she didn't dare pull that crap when she was locked up in Riker's Island, in New York.

"Why not?" I ask.

"New York girls are rough; they will slice and dice you up with the quickness."

Toi is addicted to expensive designer clothes, so she's in here for using unauthorized credit cards to purchase those types of material things.

Sierra, a bona fide crackhead, is another inmate I become fast friends with, even though she's not from New York. She was arrested for something related to crack.

She tells me all about her life before crack. She tells me she has a child and that she's the wife to an affluent white man who's threatening to leave her if she doesn't get her act together.

She shows me pictures of how she used to look before crack jacked her up. I can't believe what I am seeing. The woman I'm sitting next to is undernourished. She has black patches around sunken eyes that make her look like a raccoon. Her hair and dark skin are desiccated; however, the woman in the pictures is healthy looking and well-dressed as she poses in front of a big fancy house.

"Wow!" I say. "Is that you? You look good, girl. Is that your house? You are living large, girl."

"Yes, but my husband is sick of me. If I don't stop getting high, I'm going to lose him and my kid."

Sierra's time at the county jail is cut short when, one day in the wee hours, she's transported to the big house: prison.

Week four

Another public defender, Duana Sanson, is assigned to my case. Thank goodness! The first counsel sucked badly. I got this strange feeling she was not on my team. She was a bit too chummy with Detective Buice, who is clearly not on my side. If you ask me, they were in cahoots. I peeped how they were flirting with each other at my first court hearing where I was charged with aggravated assault, which is punishable from one year up to twenty years; my bail was set at ten thousand dollars, and a no-contact-with-the-victim was ordered.

Duana is a pretty, dark-haired, young Caucasian; she's very pleasant, too. I sense she's on my team. She informs me the prosecutor is requesting I serve three years in prison.

"Three years?" I cry.

"Yes. But that's not all. They are also requesting two years on probation after you serve three years in prison. So that's a total of five years.

"Five years?"

"Yes. But I'm going to request a bail reduction, and I'm going to see if I can get your felony dropped to a misdemeanor."

I like Duana as a person, but I get the feeling she's new to the law game, possibly fresh out of law school. She seems somewhat timid and rather unrefined. But she'll have to do until someone bails me out.

Week five

No one has come to bail me out. What's up with that? Don't my family know I'm at my wits' end in this zoo? I call Millie collect to remind her that one thousand dollars—ten percent of ten thousand—is all she'll need to scrape up to get me out.

"We're gathering the money together, Fluffy," Millie tells me. "Your sister should be down at the jail within a day or two to bail you out. Hang in there!"

CHAPTER 27

Month two

My sister pays me a visit; she tells me they're still trying to raise the thousand dollars needed to bail me out. Donations come in from a few sources, but after a few weeks of collecting money, Millie tells me they spent the currency they raised (instead of returning it to the contributors) because they didn't collect enough to bail me out.

On top of that, my public defender, Duana, is unsuccessful at getting my bail reduced and my felony dropped to a misdemeanor.

Without a real lawyer like Cochran on my side, I'm doomed! So, I tell Duana I don't want to take this case to trial because I have no chance of winning. I just want to get it over with expeditiously. "I want to plea guilty," I tell her.

Maybe, I reason, it's not time for my freedom. Maybe, if let out too soon, I'll return to Lucifer. Maybe the karmic spell, I was under or still am under, hasn't fully worn off. Maybe, just maybe, this whole jail event is some sort of intervention from the Universe, I convince myself.

Month three

While I count down the days until my next court hearing, one of my admirers, a top executive for Marriott International, I met while in New York in 1999, offers to bail me out. At first, the news excites me. I can finally be free. Then, after carefully thinking it through, I decline his kind offer after convincing myself that I'm going to be released at my next court appearance, which, according to Duana, is scheduled to take place in a few days, so why waste his hard-earned money on my foolish mess?

To pass the time until my court date, I continue to hang out in the dayroom where I sometimes play Spades, watch TV, or watch other inmates argue and fight. Other times, I lie on my cot and read the *Left Behind* series that another inmate loans me, and sometimes I corn-braid inmates' hair. I usually charge them a honey bun or a chocolate bar. Sometimes I'll accept sleeping pills as payment, too.

Meanwhile, Jeannette continues to pass her time away sleeping inside cell 301. I guess it's for the best because most of the inmates are afraid of her and try to avoid her. They just see her as some mentally deranged woman that I've yet to meet. I've only met the bright side.

"You're not afraid of her?" some of the inmates ask me.

"No," I tell them. "Why should I be?"

"She's crazy."

When Jeannette's awake, we usually spend our time hanging out by the narrow window in cell 301.

After chow time, we collect empty milk cartons; then Jeannette uses the razor I gave her to cut the milk cartons into the letters of the alphabet; then we use the carved-out letters to spell words and place them in the narrow window. This is the way we communicate with the male inmates whose windows are straight across from ours.

Spending half of the day communicating with the male inmates gives us something to do and makes the day go by quicker, despite the fact the conversation is usually smutty.

When we see the words, "*Show Me Your Pussy*" posted up in the males' narrow window, Jeannette gladly and quickly complies. She hops onto the top cot, removes her panties, and spreads her legs eagle style all up in the window. I don't have the guts to do such a thing, but it sure is entertaining watching this freak show.

When it's our turn, we spell: "*Show Me Your Dick,*" and just like Jeannette, the male inmates whip out their weenies and before you know it there's a row of sausages, every flavor and size, lined up in the narrow windows. One dick is so big and black it instantly becomes famous. The female inmates are going berserk over this anaconda, and so it hangs out in its narrow window often, entertaining us female inmates. As time goes by, the prisoner with the big black dick receives fan mail from some of the horny female inmates, too.

Now that I look back on it, I wonder if that big, black, famous cock belonged to Nicki Minaj's ex-boyfriend and hype man, Safaree Samuels. Things that make you go hmmm.

Of course, this kind of activity is not allowed in jail, so, we usually have an inmate post up somewhere in the dayroom to be on the lookout for the guards. When the lookout inmate informs us that the on-duty officer is entering our pod, we quickly take down the milk carton letters—which are considered contraband—and hide them under a pillow or inside a sneaker or inside our commissary bags.

Sometimes we have surprise shakedowns: that's when a bunch of officers unexpectedly barge into our cells and turn it upside down looking for contraband. If they find and confiscate our milk carton letters, we simply collect more milk cartons during chow time, and Jeannette gets to carving out letters once again.

One day, the whole dorm is on lockdown. A black male janitor, an older man, comes inside our dorm, and when he nears cell 301, Jeannette flashes him her boobs. As he gets closer, they exchange words, and before long, the janitor is putting lots of money on Jeannette's books. And as the caring person I know her to be, she is more than happy to return the favor and buys me gobs of junk food on commissary day.

Month four

Jeannette finally decides to hang out in the dayroom with me, but she gets into a verbal dispute with another inmate. Because of Jeannette's violent history, the on-duty officer informs Jeannette's rival to come out of the pod before the situation escalates.

Later that evening while all inmates are locked in their cells for Count, Jeannette is still steaming, and she starts yelling to the inmate she had argued with earlier. "Imma fuck you up when they open the doors!"

Jeannette doesn't let up threatening to do bodily harm to the other inmate. So finally, afraid for the other inmate's life, the on-duty officer tells Jeannette to pack up all her stuff because she's going to move Jeannette to another pod. Jeannette doesn't want us to part, so she refuses to pack up.

The on-duty female officer is afraid of Jeannette, too, so she calls for backup. Within moments, two big linebacker-looking male officers show up. As one of them grabs Jeannette's ankles, the other one holds her arms, and like a log, they carry her out of pod 300. Jeannette doesn't leave in silence; she screams and yells obscenities at the officers the whole excursion to the other side, the southeast side of the jail.

Now that my bodyguard is gone, I'm feeling a tad worried. Who's going to protect me if a big tough bully is thrown in cell 301 with me?

I'm tired of struggling to get on the top cot. There's no ladder, so I have to step on the bottom cot and leap onto the top. I quickly move to the bottom cot before a new inmate joins me. It isn't long after Jeannette's eviction from pod 300, another inmate moves in with me. Bummer! I was enjoying cell 301 all to myself.

My new cellmate has a horrendous odor flowing out of her vaginal area. Smells like a rat crawled in it and died—pee-ew!

"Why do you smell like that?" I ask my new smelly celly.

"I just had an abortion," she tells me.

I don't believe her, but whatever her issue, I decide she's got to go. I can't do this scent another moment. Now I understand what Jeannette meant when she told me she didn't tolerate stink smelling cellmates living in a tiny room with her.

I notice my new cellmate has a friend on the top tier who just so happens to have a cell all to herself. Bingo! I convince my new celly to move upstairs into the cell with her friend. She agrees, and my problem is solved—whew!

For a whole week after smelly celly's departure, I have cell 301 all to myself and then in walks another new cellmate; she stinks, too. Oh brother, here we go again! This stringy-haired brunette tells me she's a crack addict and is happy to be here. She'd been in the streets for days getting high.

"I'm tired and hungry," she tells me. "I hope they keep me here for a while, so I can get some rest."

I don't have to smell her funk for too long because she goes into the day room where the two shower stalls are located. She hops in one of the stalls—thank goodness—and washes her dirty, oily hair and smelly pale-pink body.

Two days later, an officer comes to our cell and yells at my celly, "Pack it up! You can go home now."

"Nooooo!" she cries out. "I'm not ready to leave!"

"Would you like to trade places with me?" I jokingly say.

"How much time you got?"

"I haven't been sentenced yet, but I'm facing up to twenty years. You're welcome to switch places with me."

She declines and reluctantly exits cell 301, leaving me shocked and amazed to know there are people in this world who'd rather be in jail than out there in the cold mean streets.

After her departure, a whole hour hasn't even gone by before the inmate in the next cell—cell 302—asks me if she can move into cell 301 with me. She tells me she's afraid to be in a cell all alone. I'm not scared. In fact, I prefer being in a cell by myself—fewer problems. I tell her, "No. I want to be alone."

I do not pay any attention to the fear in her voice or her emotional state, not until I hear her screaming and banging on her cell door. "Open the door!" she yells. "Let me out of here! Help meeee!"

The on-duty officer rushes to her aid. As she's escorted out of cell 302, I notice blood seeping through the towel wrapped around her wrist. Now I'm feeling a tad awful for not extending a helping hand in her time of despair. Maybe, just maybe, a few minutes of my time could have changed her outlook about her situation.

Hopefully—no thanks to me—she'll get the help she needs in the suicide watch pod where she'll be monitored around the clock.

CHAPTER 28

Surprisingly, I've been in cell 301 by myself for several weeks now. I also have a few admirers now that Jeannette's out of the way. Some of the bull-daggers stop by my cell from time to time to see what I'm all about. There's this one annoying inmate, Kimberly. Every single morning she's up bright and early banging on my cell door.

"Go away!" I tell her each time. I roll my eyes and suck my teeth at her and turn over in my bed to try to finish my dream. That does no good, though; she continues to pursue me.

When I hang out in the dayroom, she follows me everywhere. I can't seem to get away from her. Everywhere I turn, there she is, in my face trying to persuade me to bull-dag with her.

"I'm not gay!" I tell her repeatedly. "I like men; leave me alone!"

Whatever I say to her goes in one ear and straight out the other, and like clockwork, she continues to hunt me down. Finally, I stop speaking to her altogether. I completely ignore her. It works. For a period of time, she leaves me alone. But it doesn't last too long before she's back in my face. So, this time I give in and allow her access to my cell one morning after breakfast to see what she got to talk about. While I'm sitting on the bottom cot, she leans down and kisses me smack dab on my lips. Afterward, I feel a crumb or something she left on my lips, so I wipe my lips with the back of my hand and what do I find? A big clunk of grits she had for breakfast—yuck.

Another time she barges into my cell and tackles me on to my bed. While I'm flat on my back, she jumps on top of me and begins humping.

"Get off!" I yell, pushing her away. I consider ignoring her again. Then I just do it. I stop speaking to her once again, but this time for good.

Bummer! I finally get another cellmate. She looks like a boy. She's been transferred from the southeast side where Jeannette is.

"Is your name Vanessa?" she asks me.

"Yeah, why?"

"Jeannette was my cellmate on the southeast side. She told me she's going to fuck me up if I mess with you."

We both bust out laughing.

My new cellmate gives me no problems, thanks to Jeannette, possibly. And then two days later she's released.

For the past several days, inmate Sandra Hubbard has been asking me if she can be my bunkmate. I know before long another inmate will be thrown into the cell with me; and ain't no telling what she'll be like. She could be another smelly celly or maybe that burly dyke I'd envisioned when I first arrived here. With that thought swimming around in my head, I decide to finally take Sandra up on her offer. She came to pod 300 three months after my arrival, so, we've grown pretty close to one another. And she's cool beans.

Although swapping and switching cells is against the rules, who cares? Inmates never obey jail rules; so, when the on-duty officer isn't paying attention—that's right, Sandra's swap is a success.

According to Sandra, she's a black woman trapped inside an attractive, pale-pink, skinny, blue-eyed blond body. You cannot tell her she isn't an African American.

"I hate white people," she says to me one day.

"Excuse me? I hate to bust your bubble, but you're white, Sandra."

"No, I'm not. For real, for real."

"What you are," I chuckle, "is delusional."

Sandra has a black pimp who visits her once a week and leaves ten dollars on her books every time. No more, no less.

"My daughter is coming to see me today," she says. "She's black."

I chuckle again. "Stop lying, Sandra."

"Yes, she is black. Wait and see. She'll be here soon."

I wait, and sho nuff' Sandra's daughter is a kinky-haired, dark-skinned, 18-year-old.

"She's pretty, Sandra," I say. "and she's black."

"I told you she's black. I told you!"

Although I didn't ask, I wonder if Sandra's Jheri-curl wearing pimp is her daughter's father.

Sandra loves to dance. Every day she stands underneath the TV in the dayroom and puts on a show. Her rhythmless performances are side-splitting. But more than dancing, Sandra loves spending hours in the narrow window talking to one of the male inmates by means of the milk carton letters. He's black, of course, and she swears she's in love with him. When she's not in the window, she spends a lot of time sitting on the top cot writing love letters to him. Sandra somehow was able to drop out of school in the fifth grade, so she's illiterate. She can barely read and write, but with my assistance, she successfully writes letters to her new man and mail them to him every day.

Eventually, her letter writing takes its toll on me. It's beginning to feel as though I'm writing her long letters instead of her and that's not how I want to spend my time in jail. I can't even read a book in peace without Sandra interrupting me to ask me to spell words.

"I'm not gonna spend all day spelling words for you, Sandra," I snap one day. "Get a dictionary!"

Sandra buys a dictionary from the commissary, but it doesn't solve her issue—duh. Silly me. Sandra can't find the words in the dictionary because she can't read.

"Daggonit, Sandra! Sound it out," I snap. "I'm tired of spelling words for you all day long. If you can't spell, then don't write any more letters!"

CHAPTER 29

Month six.

Something strange is happening to me as I sit in a small room across from my pod. It's the place I go whenever I want to break the monotony and hook up with Jeannette. It's like our meeting spot.

The room is filled with inmates from other pods. We are sitting circled around a woman minister who's here to share the good news about her lord and savior, Jesus. I am sure her sermon is powerful, but I'm not paying attention to her. The boyish-looking inmate sitting straight across from me has my attention today. Her legs are spread open the way men usually sit. Her hair, or lack thereof, is shaved close to her head, nearly bald.

I recognize her. She's the hall monitor, the special inmate who's allowed out of her pod every day, all day, to assist the on-duty correction officers. She's favored by all of them, too. As the hall monitor, she gets to enjoy all the advantages and privileges denied the rest of the inmates.

This must be her first time attending one of these church services. I wonder why she decided to join us today. I never paid much attention to her until now. I examine every inch of her—feet to head—and I wonder if she's really a female.

My eyes make their way up to her smooth, dark-brown pretty face. And then I look into her eyes through the glasses she's wearing. She catches me staring at her. She gazes back. I feel myself lusting after her in the same way I've lusted after a man and wonder what's come over me.

When service is over, I say goodbye to Jeannette who must return to her side of the jail and then I walk on over to Miss Hall Monitor, or shall I say Mister Hall Monitor? After all, that's what she's posing as: a man, a mister.

"Hello. How you doin'?" I say when I approach her. "I'm Vanessa. What's your name?"

"Yolanda. But everybody calls me Yo-Yo."

"What pod you stay in?"

"Four hundred. And you?"

"Three hundred." I hear the on-duty officer order all inmates back inside their assigned pods. "Nice meeting you, Yo-Yo," I say before walking away.

"Nice meeting you, too, Vanessa."

I feel Yo-Yo watching me as I walk inside pod 300.

Later that evening, Jeannette is whisked off to prison to serve the rest of her one year sentence. We didn't get a chance to say bye-bye to each other, and I don't even know which prison she's going to.

The next morning, after breakfast, I sit down on my cot and write Yo-Yo a short love letter. At the end, instead of signing my name, I write "*With love, cell 301.*"

By the afternoon, I spot Yo-Yo mopping the hall, so I tell my cellmate Sandra to slip her the letter. "Don't tell her it's from me," I say.

Sandra slides the letter under the front door while I pretend I'm totally into the game of Spades I'm playing with some of the other inmates. Yo-Yo sets the mop aside, picks up the folded letter, and reads it. Afterward, I watch as her eyes zoom in on cell 301. I chuckle to myself when I realize she has no clue the letter is from me, Miss Cell 301.

Every day, for the next few days, Sandra slips Yo-Yo a letter from me, and each time, I close with, "*With love, cell 301.*"

Eventually, Yo-Yo figures out I'm Miss Cell 301 and, she writes me back, then I write her back, and so on and so forth. Before long we're secret pen pals. It's a secret because Yo-Yo has a girlfriend living with her in pod 400, a girl who's also her codefendant.

In due course, Yo-Yo wants to spend private time with me, so in one of her letters, she explains how I am to meet her in the mop closet that's out in the hall, near the control booth. "Make like you accidentally spilled water on the floor in your cell," Yo-Yo writes. "The officer will let you out of your pod to get the mop."

Once inside the mop closet, Yo-Yo joins me, and I give her a peck-kiss and a hug. When rec time rolls around, Yo-Yo and I can be found together in the gym shooting hoops. To my surprise, Yo-Yo sucks at basketball, and I win every time.

Now that I have Yo-Yo, life in jail isn't as boring, and every morning when my Maker wakes me up, I look forward to seeing Yo-Yo peering inside my pod looking for me. We wave, blow kisses, and pass along our love letters.

CHAPTER 30

Month eight, April 4, 2000

A constant clicking sound jolts me awake. "*Click, click, click, click, click.*" It's the on-duty correctional officer unlocking my door, and the extra clicks are to wake me out of my sleep before the crack of dawn.

"Vanessa Murray!" she yells out through the loudspeaker from the control booth. "Get up and get dressed! You're going to court."

Today is judgment day! It's the moment I've been waiting for since the day I was arrested. I pray I hear the judge say, "Time served! You're free to go home, young lady."

I quickly jump out of bed, brush my teeth, wash my face, and throw on my ugly, wrinkled two-piece orange jail suit over my two-piece white long johns I bought from the commissary; afterward, I slide on a new pair of white cotton socks, then lace up my blood-spattered sneakers, before placing my feet into them.

I'm excited and jumpy as a virgin at a prison rodeo. I'm excited because I'm finally going to hear the judge's

State Property

verdict. Not knowing is a far more nerve-racking ordeal than knowing, even if it's bad news.

I'm jumpy because, for the past several weeks, inmates have been warning me about the judge presiding over my case.

"They call him Hanging Hancock," inmates tell me.

"Why?" I ask.

"He's real mean. He gave his own son ten years for selling drugs. I feel sorry for you. You better pray for another judge."

"What does he look like?" I ask. "Is he a white racist?"

"No. He's black...black, old, mean, and he has gray hair."

To make matters worse, my public defender, Duana, agrees when I ask her if what the inmates have been telling me about Judge Hancock true.

"I'm going to see if I can get you another judge," Duana tells me. Her idea of another judge is a white judge, and I'm not too sure that's a good idea, especially if he's a racist. But still, I spent the last few weeks praying that mean, old, gray-headed Hancock is too sick to show up; but in case he does, I create plan B: a letter begging Hanging Hancock to have mercy on my tender soul. I gave the handwritten letter to Duana the last time she'd visited me in jail.

"Please be sure to give this letter to my judge before my court date," I told her.

"I will," Duana promised.

"Let's go, inmate Murray," yells the correctional officer from the control booth.

"I'm coming," I yell back.

"Good luck," a half-sleeping Sandra tells me.

"Thanks."

I scurry to the front of the pod and stand at the door as I wait for the correctional officer to pop open the door to let me out.

"Where do you think you're going with sneakers on?" the officer asks me. "You can't wear sneakers to court."

"Why not?"

"Because you might try to escape and with sneakers on you just might outrun us."

I scamper back to cell 301 and put on my worn-out plastic brown ugly flip flops. I walk back to the front of the pod and when I hear the door click, I open it and line up in the hallway with the other nervous inmates scheduled for sentencing today, too.

Amid the inmates lined up against a wall, all wearing orange, I spot Yo-Yo in the line. Boy, am I happy to see her. The big grin on her face tells me she's happy to see me, too. I squeeze into line right behind her and instantly I can sense she, too, is as jumpy as a virgin at a prison rodeo. Like me, she's charged with a felony. She arrived at this county jail roughly two weeks before me. She too is facing many years behind bars except, unlike mine, her charge or charges are for armed robbery and kidnapping.

State Property

"You have a bachelor's in biology," I say to Yo-Yo the very first time she told me her reason for being here. "Why in the world would you rob a chicken joint and abduct the workers? What is wrong with you?"

Yo-Yo giggled at my reaction and response and then gave me some lame reason for committing that kind of crime. This isn't her first offense, either. She's served time in Fulton County Jail, too, for selling drugs, she told me.

A correctional officer approaches our line with a couple of long transport chains with multiple cuffs attached to them. One of the long chains is used to connect multiple prisoners wrist to wrist, and the other long chain she uses to cuff our ankles. I'm standing next to Yo-Yo, so her wrist is cuffed to mine.

Once we are all cuffed up nice and good, the female officer crams all of us inside an elevator which takes us to the first floor, where we wait for a young, black sheriff to drive us to court.

I recognize this sheriff, and he remembers me, too. He's the same one who took me to court months ago for a different hearing. He's the same one who had placed me in the elevator alone with him, and as the elevator took us to the first floor, he thought it would be a good idea to touch my booty while my hands were cuffed in front. I felt helpless and did nothing but yell out, "Heeey!"

Today, I'm not alone, but that doesn't stop him from flirting with me as he loads us into a large white prison van, then drives us straight to the courthouse in Decatur, Georgia.

On the way there, I notice my homegirl, Angie, crossing the street. She works in the neighborhood so I'm not too surprised to see her, but what a coincidence. Then again, she knows I'm scheduled to appear in court today. I wonder if she's heading to the courthouse. It saddens me, nonetheless, that she doesn't even know I'm one of the criminals wearing ankle and wrist shackles in the prison van that passes her by.

As soon as we enter the courthouse building, the sheriff throws us into one large holding cell with cinderblock walls and cold metal benches pinned to a concrete floor, then he removes the chain gang cuffs and tells us we'll have to wait our turn to see the judge assigned to our case.

Inside the holding cell, I take a break from conversing with Yo-Yo and strike up a conversation with another inmate who has sorrow written all over her face. Like me, and many other inmates I've met, she doesn't look like a criminal. She looks to be in her early 20s and she's very attractive with eyes the color of a ripe hazelnut.

"What are you here for?" I ask Hazelnut Eyes.

"Murder."

"Murder? Ohmygod! Who did you kill?"

"My lover."

"You killed your boyfriend?"

State Property

"No, my girlfriend. I stabbed her to death. I'm charged with manslaughter."

"How much time are you facing?"

"Twenty five years, fifteen in prison."

"Wow!"

"What about you?" she asks me.

"Well, the judge can give me up to twenty years, but the prosecution recommended five years: three in prison and two on probation," I tell her. "but I'm hoping the judge overrule their recommendation and release me today."

"I wish I was only facing five years," she says.

My heart goes out to her as she tells me all about the day she fatally stabbed her allegedly abusive girlfriend while they were fighting. She seems like such a sweet girl who made a tragic mistake or, as I like to call it, a bad choice as in my case, too. She also tells me she has a young son, around 6 years old. My heart goes out to him. He'll be a grown man by the time she's released.

After sitting in that holding cell for a couple hours, mine, Yo-Yo's, and a couple other inmates' names are finally called at the same time. We're cuffed again and escorted to different courtrooms for our different cases.

On the right and left sides of the courtroom I'm assigned to are pew-style wooden benches. There are tables at the front of the wooden benches, on both sides. Water pitchers and plastic cups sit on the tables. At the front of the courtroom, facing the pews, is a raised desk, but no judge is sitting there. Adjacent to the judge's seat is an empty witness stand and nearby, at a smaller desk, sits a court reporter.

A young black bailiff escorts me to the pew on the right side and then he stands against the wall. Soon after, spectators and parties or witnesses to the cases to be presented today enter the courtroom.

Well, well, well! Look who's here. It's my friend, Angie. I guess she was on her way here after all. I'm so happy to see her. She's the only person in that courtroom there for me. She takes a seat on the benches on the left side. She sees me and waves. I smile and wave back. The bailiff notices.

"Who's that?" the nosy bailiff asks me.

"My sister," I lie, thinking only family members are allowed inside the courtroom because that's what an inmate told me.

"She's pretty," the bailiff tells me. "I'll be right back. I want to talk to your sister."

While the bailiff is chopping it up with Angie, I spot my antagonist as she enters the courtroom. She's with one of Lucifer's flunkies. She sees me, too, and rolls her eyes. I roll mine right back at her.

Oh boy! Here she comes. Out of all the places she can sit, she walks over to the benches on the right side and takes a seat a few rows behind me. After a few minutes, I feel someone breathing hot air on my neck. I quickly turn my head around only to find out it's her: my angry antagonist trying to start mess with me.

She's annoying me. Yes, I want to pop her in her head, but I, at least, have enough sense to know that's not going to help my case. So, instead of bopping her forehead with mine, I give her and the flunky one of those looks that says, 'you better not try me while my back is turned,' then I roll my eyes at both of them and turn back around to face the front of the courtroom.

Where's my bailiff? I see him still talking to Angie. I hope he hurries and makes his way back on this side of the courtroom before my adversary does something stupid like punch me in the back of my head.

At last! The bailiff makes his way back over to my side of the room and posts himself back up against the wall facing me.

"I thought you said Angie is your sister?" he asks me.

"She is. She's my spiritual sister," I say, then quickly change the subject. "So, where's the judge?"

After what seems like a long wait, a black man wearing a black robe walks through a door behind the raised desk. I wonder if that's Hanging Hancock. No way. It can't be. He looks so young. Except for the fact that he's black, he looks nothing like the inmates' description of him. I search for the gray hairs, but I don't see any. I try to find a mean streak in his face; I see none. It isn't until he sits behind the raised desk, I notice the inscription on the nameplate on his desk: Michael E. Hancock. That's him! That's my judge.

After calling a few cases before mine, Hancock looks my way and points at me; then I overhear him say to the assistant prosecuting attorney, a petite black woman, "Is she the one who did the stabbing?"

I detect a look of surprise on his face when the assistant prosecutor says, "Yes, that's her." His facial expression tells me I look nothing like a ratchet dimwitted fool, the role I played eight months ago on that balmy summer evening.

It's amazing how someone's countenance and body language can tell you a whole lot about them without them saying much or anything. Take Beyoncé's mother, Tina Knowles-Lawson, for instance. You know that humiliating incident, when she got on national television and, straight to her fine-looking husband's face, she rolled her eyes and told him (accomplished actor and survivor of a plane crash), he was not perfect, although she'd prayed to God for a new man to go along with her new car and new city. The look on Mr. Richard Lawson's face told many viewers, who'd watched the video that went viral, he wasn't pleased with the way his wife "labeled" the man she'd wished for, cataloging him a defective husband right after she'd praised herself.

Judge Hancock calls my name. The nosy bailiff escorts me to the front of the courtroom, then steps aside. Sitting on the left side of the courtroom in the front pew is my public defender, Duana. I quickly walk toward her, and she tells me to sit down next to her.

"Would you like some water?" she asks me.

"No, thank you," I tell her, and then I lean in and whisper, "Did you give him my letter?"

"Yes," she whispers back. Then she tells me she had no luck getting a different judge. I'm not surprised and happy she didn't. I like Hancock. His energy feels good. I can sense that he has sort of a soft spot for me. "Are you sure you don't want to take this case to trial?" Duana asks.

"Will I get more than five years if I lose?" I often heard inmates say if you lose at your trial you're guaranteed to get sentenced to double the original time that was recommended by the prosecution.

"Perhaps," Duana says.

"I'll stick with the guilty plea."

Why would I take this case to trial when I've already admitted I cut the girl? What sense does it make to jeopardize a five-year sentence for ten or more? I realize Duana is not too bright. Plus, she did not have enough ammunition to get my bail reduced; nor did she have enough to get my felony reduced to a misdemeanor; nor was she able to get a different judge to preside over my case. So, why in the world would I expect this inexperienced lawyer to have enough ammo to win my case at a trial? How preposterous is that?

After the judge hears the arguments from both the defense (Duana) and prosecution, Duana asks me if I'd like to speak on my own behalf before the judge imposes the sentence. I choose not to because as far as I'm concern, my letter spoke for me.

The judge asks Angie to approach the front of the courtroom to give her description of my true nature. She informs the judge that she doesn't know me to be violent or confrontational and as she walks back to her seat, she stops next to me to tell me that Hancock was the same judge that had presided over her first divorce case.

Next and last, the so-called victim, my antagonist, is called to the front of the courtroom to tell her version of what had transpired on the day in question.

"Look what she did to me!" she cries out in anger as she points at the scar I'd created on the upper part of her left arm, a gash that required several stitches. "All we were doing was arguing and she went overboard!"

"How much time do you think she should spend in jail?" Hancock asks her.

"Forever!"

"Why?" Hancock asks. "She doesn't strike me as a violent person."

"Because I have to wear this scar forever!"

I could tell by the look on Hancock's face he isn't buying her spiel when she tries to convince him, and everyone in the courtroom, that she's afraid of me. And as she speaks about her relationship with Lucifer and how he comforted her (only when the police appeared on the scene), and how I didn't even call her from jail to apologize to her, and how I am the one who interfered in their relationship—not the other way around, and I was disloyal to her—not Lucifer, and I, I, I.

It was all my fault, according to her, even though Lucifer set the stage for this mess, and she and I were dumb enough to join him on stage. So, as far as I'm concerned, we are looking like two stupid idiots standing in court, delusional about a man who didn't even show up in support of either one of us.

"Here's what I'm going to do," Hancock says. "Instead of three years in prison, I'm going to give you two years in prison and three years on probation."

"My client has been incarcerated for eight months thus far; will she get credit for those eight months?" Duana asks.

"Yes." Hancock replies.

I'm a tad disappointed I must remain behind bars for another year and four months; however, I'm relieved and thankful a twenty year prison term wasn't imposed on me—whew!

Hanging Hancock does, after all, have a tiny soft spot in his heart for me, no matter what those inmates said about him. In my book, he's no Hanging Hancock. He's Compassionate Hancock.

Back in cuffs once again, I'm led out of the courtroom back to the holding cell where I anxiously await the verdicts of some of the other inmates who rode in the prison van with me. I'm especially anxious to know the amount of time Yo-Yo must serve, if any.

I wait about an hour before the other inmates return to the holding cell. Yo-Yo and Hazelnut Eyes aren't as fortunate as I am.

Yo-Yo is sentenced to ten years; she must serve six years in prison and the rest on parole. Hazelnut Eyes is sentenced to twenty five years and must serve fifteen years in prison and the rest on parole.

It breaks my heart to know they'll be spending that much time incarcerated because after getting to know both women, I can discern that they're not bad-to-the-bone people, especially Yo-Yo.

Like many people on this planet, they're victims of their own inner demon, and like me, they're now on a path to making choices they can celebrate and not regret.

CHAPTER 31

May 22, 2000

"Vanessa Murray, pack it up!" yells the on-duty officer from the control booth. I jump out of bed and notice it's one-thirty in the wee hours.

It's been nearly seven weeks to the day I was sentenced. I don't have to ask what's going on. Everybody knows that when an officer yells, "Pack it up!" you're either going home or to prison. I still have over a year left to serve, so I know I'm not going home.

A few hours earlier, May 21st, I celebrated my thirty-eighth birthday in a quiet corner of my cell, where the chocolate cupcake I bought from the commissary was my make-believe birthday cake. "Happy birthday to me," I quietly sang to myself before making a wish and shoving the cake down my throat.

"Hurry up, inmate Murray!"

"I'm coming!" I yell to the officer. Then I turn to Sandra, who's now awake, and whisper, "If she keeps that up, she's gonna wake the dead."

I throw my books, pictures, and love letters from Yo-Yo in my commissary bag. Then I hug a teary-eyed Sandra before leaving my cell.

"I'mma miss you, Vanessa," Sandra calls out as I walk to the front of the pod. "You better write me and let me know what prison they stick you in."

"Okay, I will."

The squad car ride to Metro State Prison in Atlanta takes about fifteen minutes. When we pull up in front of the prison, the male officer gets out the driver seat, opens the back door of his squad car and assists me and another inmate out the back seat, then he removes our cuffs from our wrists before leaving us with two female correctional officers.

As we're walking toward the barbed wire facility, I spot Yo-Yo behind the wired fence. She was shipped here five days ago. Sporting a white jumpsuit and black combat boots, she's marching in line and singing military cadences with a bunch of other inmates in the same getup.

State Property

"Yo' left, yo' left, yo' left, right, left," they chant. "Everywhere I go (everywhere I go), there's a C.O. watching me (there's a C.O. watching me) ..."

"What is this, the army?" I whisper to the inmate who rode in the same squad car with me.

"I know. Right. What the hell is this shit?" she whispers back. We giggle like two class clowns.

"You think this is funny?" one of the female officers yells, looking in my direction.

"No," I say, looking sheepish.

She moves in close to me. "When I ask you a question, inmate, your response should be 'Ma'am, no, ma'am' or 'Ma'am, yes, ma'am.' Is that understood, inmate?"

"Yes, sir…oops, I mean, yes, ma'am." I look at the other inmate and see her struggling to suppress a snicker, which causes me to burst out laughing in the officer's face.

"I see you don't follow directions very well, inmate!" She moves in closer, our noses nearly touching. I feel her hot breath on my face. "Are you eyeballing me, inmate?"

"No," I say.

"No what?" she screams. "Did we already forget how to address an officer?"

"No, ma'am...I mean, Ma'am, no, ma'am."

We finally end up inside the prison grounds behind the barbed wire fence. The guard commands me and the other inmate to join a few other new arrivals who are standing in line and then she escorts us into a building where more officers are awaiting our arrival.

"If you got braids, twists, or locks in your hair, take 'em out now!" shouts an officer. "And make it quick, before I cut your hair off!"

"I just got my hair braided yesterday," I whisper to one of the other arrivals standing next to me.

The front half of my hair is in tiny cornrows going back, while the back part is twisted in two strands. With the help of another new arrival, I unbraid some of my cornrows and untwists my two strands. Now I look disheveled.

"Take off your clothes!" shouts a female prison guard.

"Everything?" I ask.

"Yes, take it all off, inmate. And put it in here." She hands me a big black garbage bag. I place my orange county jail suit, panties, and bra inside the bag then set the bag aside. Whatever dignity I walked in here with is stripped off with my clothes.

I cross my arms over my small boobs to cover up some of the humiliation. Then the guard tells me to squat and cough while she points her flashlight up my butthole and down my throat and takes a thorough look inside.

Afterward, she hoses me down with a sticky fluid that smells sort of like roach spray. She sprays the fluid in my hair and on my hairy yoni. "Lift up your arms," she says. "Straight up, like this." She sprays the sticky stuff onto my armpits. I try hard to hold back the tears welling up in my eyes as she hands me a small bar of soap and instructs me to stand in a doorless shower stall. "Wash your hair," she says, "and hurry up! You only get two minutes."

Two minutes is not enough time to properly wash and rinse away the sticky stuff, but I do the best I can under the circumstances; then I dry off with the towel she hands me.

"Here," she says, "put these on." She hands me a white jumpsuit, the same kind I saw Yo-Yo marching in, along with a gray sweatshirt, a huge pair of bloomers, and a huge bra that looks like a size 44DDD. In a huff, I shove the bra and bloomers back at her.

"I'm not putting on these nasty things!" I shout at her. "They're dirty, and they're not even my size."

"Yes, you are putting them on!" she yells back.

"No! I'm not! These panties have piss stains on them, and the bra is dingy. That's unsanitary. I'm not putting them on."

"Yes, you are!"

"No! I'm not! Can I just put back on the panty and bra I wore here?"

"No! Put on what I gave you!"

Fortunately for me, the guard turns her back to address another matter. I swiftly grab the black bag and search inside it for the clean panty and bra I wore here. Found it! Then I throw the corroded undergarments in the bag and then quickly slide on the gray sweatshirt and white jumpsuit seconds before the guard turns back to me—whew! That was a close call.

She gives me a pair of black combat boots and while my hair is still wet and sticky, she instructs me to sit in front of a camera as another prison guard snaps photographs of me.

CHAPTER 32

Metro State Prison[4] is not only a maximum-security facility for women; it's also Georgia's Diagnostic and Classification facility for women or better yet, it's an intense boot camp style facility, which entails marching and undergoing drills and whatnot. It's the first stop from the county jail before permanent placement at one of the four women's prisons in Georgia.

Upon arrival, each new inmate, called a diagnostic inmate, is given a handbook of regulations and is thoroughly instructed on the rules of prison life. There's also medical examinations and psychological tests to be had that last approximately three weeks while a diagnostic inmate, longer if you're found to have medical or psychological issues. Diagnostic inmates must wear white, while general population (GP) inmates dress in beige.

One of the main rules is learning how to properly address a prison employee, which I learned before I entered the barbed wires. Then there's learning how to march and

---

[4] Metro State Prison closed its doors in 2011.

sing corny military cadences made up by inmates: "Yo' left, yo' left, yo' left, right, left...I used to wear my Tommy Hills, but now they got me doing drills...."

My day starts at the crack of dawn. First things first, officers go around to each dorm and count each inmate. This is called Count. Count takes place multiple times throughout the day. Count time is to make sure no one has escaped since the last Count.

After the first headcount, I quickly change out of my pajamas and into my white jumpsuit and black combat boots and head outside and join the rest of the inmates in a single file line. Once all inmates are lined up properly, we march and belt out the corny cadences all the way to the chow hall where the first meal of the day is served.

We're given roughly 10 minutes to stuff our breakfast down our throats before being told to get up and leave the chow hall. After chow time, inmates are patted down to make sure we didn't steal any food or utensils, then we march and sing our way back to the dorm. Once back at the dorm, it's time to clean the whole dorm from top to bottom.

I've never been in the armed forces, but I imagine this is what it must be like, to some extent, which by the way I am growing accustomed to. If there's one thing I can say about myself, I'm highly adaptable to change, but I'm sure that can be attributed to the fact that my sun and moon zodiac signs are mutable.

Cleaning entails dusting down everything in the dorm and mopping, waxing, and buffing floors, then making sure beds are properly made, neat and tight, and making sure toilet papers are folded a certain kind of silly way—trivial!

After we spend all morning cleaning the entire dorm, it's inspection time. The members of the inspection team wear white gloves, and they go around swiping down the prison furniture with their gloves. If a speck of dust or dirt is found on any one of the inspector's white gloves, the inmates with the dirty room are charged with a disciplinary infraction.

Once, because I didn't remember all the stupid rules, I received an infraction for having a picture of my daughter hanging up in my cubby. My punishment entailed doing a few jumping jacks outside in the hot sun—stupid!

After inspection is approved and cleared, the rest of the afternoon is spent outside marching around in circles and learning new cadences. On days we're scheduled for medical or psychological testing, we must march and sing to the testing sites.

All this marching has got me wishing I woulda served the rest of my two-year sentence at the county jail instead of this place. At least at Dekalb County Jail, I didn't have to march and sing all day. In fact, if I chose to, I didn't have to do anything but lay up in my cell and sleep my time away or read books or hang out in the day room and play Spades or watch TV.

Classification is the final stage of Diagnostic. It takes place immediately after all the medical and psychological examinations have been conducted. Inmates are assigned to a security level between one and five. Level one is trusty security. At this level, inmates have been proven trustworthy and cooperative and are therefore allowed to work for limited amounts of time without immediate supervision. The next levels are two (minimum), three (medium), four (close), and five (maximum).

Because of the nature of my crime, I'm assigned the highest level: five. Inmates at the maximum level are considered dangerous and violent, requiring supervision at all times.

Kelly Gissendaner[5], a Caucasian woman, is sitting on death row. She's the only woman in the state of Georgia serving a death sentence. She's kept in solitary caging all day, although I did see her on the grounds once. She had her wrists, ankles, and her whole body in shackles as a group of correctional officers called the CERT team (Community Emergency Response Team) escorted her to one of the testing sites. All movement on the prison grounds were ordered to stop until she had passed us by as if she was a celebrity.

The word around the prison is that she's a mother of three. She's been convicted of scheming with her boyfriend to kidnap and murder her husband to get possession of a house and $20,000 in insurance money.

---

[5] Kelly Gissendaner was executed on September 30, 2015.

Her boyfriend received a life sentence with the likelihood of parole in exchange for testifying against her.

Before trial, prosecutors offered Gissendaner a plea deal of life in prison with no chance of parole for twenty five years. Like a fool, she rejected the deal. And now, she's the only woman, since 1945, that's been put to death in the state of Georgia.

From time to time, I run into Jeannette on the prison grounds. She's been here since February 21, 2000. She's already been through Diagnostic and Classification. She's now part of the general prison population right here at Metro State; instead of the white jumpsuit, she now wears a two-piece beige outfit.

The last time I see her, she tells me she'll be set free on June 2nd, which is a couple days away. She also tells me she'll be moving in with the janitor she met at DeKalb County Jail, and so she gives me his address and tells me to write her.

"I will," I promise her.

Then, just in case I don't run into her again before she sets foot in the free world, I wish her all the best.

I see Yo-Yo more regularly. Although she's not housed in my dorm, she's going through Diagnostic and Classification, too, which means we usually end up marching together to the same places and doing the same things daily. We even sit and chat together in the park during recreation time.

CHAPTER 33

June 2000

"Murray, pack it up!" yells the on-duty prison guard.

I jump out of bed and gather my belongings. For a quick second, in my sleepy state, I think I'm going home. But then I remember I still have thirteen more months to serve.

Today, I'm going to be permanently placed somewhere. Whether or not I'll stay here at Metro State Prison or at another institution, remains to be seen. I don't know why, but I pray it's not here.

When I arrive at the holding area, I'm so happy to see Yo-Yo there. This could only mean one thing: she, too, is on the schedule to join general population at one of the women's prisons. We're both hoping we end up at the same prison.

When me, Yo-Yo, and two other inmates are shackled together, ankle to ankle, like girls in a chain gang, we realize we're all going to the same prison—Pulaski State Prison.

Yo-Yo's codefendant was transported on a different day to another prison because codefendants are not allowed to serve their time at the same prison.

The two-hour ride to Hawkinsville is a welcome break after three grueling weeks of Diagnostic. During the ride in a big white van, we all laugh and crack jokes. I even get cozy enough to slide off my cuffs.

"Girl, you better put those cuffs back on," Yo-Yo whispers to me. "They could charge you with trying to escape if they see your cuffs off."

After I slide my cuffs back on, I take Yo-Yo up on her other suggestion and lie my head on her chest and catnap for the remainder of the ride.

The maximum-security facility is huge, sort of like a college campus except for the barbed wire fences. Although it's classed as a maximum-security prison, it houses female inmates of all security levels and juveniles, too.

There's one 16-year-old juvie imprisoned here for fatally shooting a man who had been molesting her; she's the only juvenile incarcerated here, but she stays in the juvie dorm alone, or until they lock up more juveniles and send them here.

As we exit the white van, an officer unshackles us and escorts us inside the prison grounds and into the check-in building. I see inmates dressed in sky blue and white uniforms going to and fro, unsupervised. I have no idea where they're going but I'm sure I'll be joining them soon.

I spot Sierra, the crackhead I befriended at DeKalb County Jail. I call out her name and she turns and gives me a wave and a smile. She looks healthy and well, nothing like she looked at the county jail. Her skin is clear; her hair is fuller and longer. I must say, prison has done wonders for her.

After check-in, me, Yo-Yo, and other new arrivals are dumped in building E9. It's very crowded and noisy up in here, but as with any situation that's thrust upon me, I'm sure I'll quickly learn to adapt to my new life as a piece of property of the state of Georgia.

Dorm E9 is one of the huge dorms which houses nearly two hundred inmates in 96 double-bunked cells. The other dorms on the prison grounds, around seven others, are bungalow style dorms so they house fewer inmates.

My first new cellmate is a white chick serving time for embezzling funds from her former job. She's quiet, clean, and minds her own business, just like me. She and I rarely talk to each other, though, and that's fine with me.

My daily work detail is night orderly. My job entails cleaning shower stalls, mopping, waxing, and buffing the huge dorm floor—no pay. Since I'm not getting paid and don't even want to be here, I purposely do a terrible job of cleaning; plus, the day orderlies will have to re-clean the whole dorm extra good in the morning because inspection takes place around 9:00 am, Monday through Friday. And here, the warden seems more concerned with making sure all the floors look shiny and new than she is with anything else.

Over time, a few of the inmates go behind my back and tell the counselor assigned to my dorm that I'm not doing a good job cleaning the shower stalls. The counselor threatens to assign me to the kitchen detail if I don't do a better job. Then she searches my face for signs of worry. I show her a look of no concern, even though I'm scared as heck to work in the kitchen. So, she changes the subject, possibly realizing that putting me to work in the kitchen where knives are stored may not be a good idea after all.

Yo-Yo is seeing another woman now. "You dumped me for that?" I jokingly say to her one day. "She looks like the back of my shoe."

Yo-Yo and I roar with laughter before she tries to explain that she's only with the shoe-face woman because she buys Yo-Yo lots of things from the commissary.

Yo-Yo and I are no longer secret lovers, or better yet, secret pen pals is more like what we were. We're simply great jail buddies now. She knows I've never been with a woman, and besides that, twat licking is not my cup of tea, whether I'd be the one giving or receiving. I'm strictly dickly, you could say. Nevertheless, I now understand how some can enter prison straight and leave gay.

After a while, Yo-Yo dumps her new girlfriend and links up with another woman.

"Much better," I tell Yo-Yo.

"I'm glad you approve of this one," she says.

"Yeah, she's pretty. She doesn't look like the back of my shoe."

CHAPTER 34

November 2000

Now that I'm nearing the end of my prison sentence with just eight more months to serve, my security level has dropped down to minimum, making me eligible for work release. But I also qualify to attend school full-time at Pulaski. A big part of me wants to stay in prison to learn a new skill: computer graphics, which will make me more marketable upon my release, and as a student, I won't have to work for free any longer. My whole day, five days a week, will be spent in a classroom with Yo-Yo who has also been accepted into the computer graphics program. She's not eligible for work release because she still has five more years to serve. You've got to have less than a year left to serve before you can do the work release program.

It's a hard decision, but I decide on the work release program. So once again, I'm cuffed and transported back to Atlanta to serve the remainder of my time at Metro Transitional Center. It's a half-way house adjacent to Metro

State Prison, which is about five miles from my sister's apartment—give or take.

I'm not adapting quickly to my new abode and new set of laws, which seems worse than prison. Shortly after I enter the building, the employees at the half-way house tell me to sit down on a bench. As soon as I sit down, they tell me to get up. As soon as I get up, they tell me to sit back down. Up, down, up, down, up, down. I finally realize this is fun and games to them, so, the next time they tell me to get up, I don't move. I remain seated.

"Stand up," they say.

I ignore them and remain seated. At this point, they can send me back to prison for all I care, but I'm not going to continue to allow them to play me like a yo-yo. I didn't come here for that.

"Get up," they tell me again. I just sit there and then I burst into tears. The center's director makes them stop. Now they're feeling sorry for me and empathize with me and comfort me, especially the director of the center, who has a son of her own currently incarcerated for selling drugs. What's worse, her son just so happens to be a famous football player, whose name I now can't recall because I've never been into football, so I wasn't a fan of his.

"Do you want to call your family?" the director asks.

"Yes," I say.

My new counselor, Ms. Pugh, escorts me into her office and phones my mother. She keeps the phone on speaker, so she can hear every word. My brother, who's been temporarily released from prison in New York, gets on the phone and says, "Hey Fluffy!"

My counselor writes down my nickname and adds it to my file. I realize talking to my family in front of my counselor is a bad idea, so I quickly end the phone call before one of them says something else my counselor doesn't need to know.

The next day isn't much better, except for the moment I see someone I know. It's crackhead Sierra. She looks even better than the last time I saw her at Pulaski State Prison. She's swathed in civilian clothes and looks nothing like an addict.

"How long have you been here?" I ask.

"About four months now," Sierra says. "I have a good job making eleven dollars an hour."

Because Sierra is one of the working residents, her living quarters are on the opposite side of the facility from nonworking residents, like me. So, I see little of her. But whenever I do see her, she slips me five dollars, so I can buy snacks and stuff from the vending machines. What a sweetie pie she is.

Photo of a 38-year-old Vanessa taken on December 8, 2000 at Metro Transitional Center located at 1303 Constitution Rd SE, Atlanta, GA 30316. This photo was taken during World of Works Graduation.

I'm still not adjusting to this place after two weeks. They still got us jumping up and down like a fireball yo-yo. No matter where we are or what we're doing, if any employee or C.O. makes an appearance, whether it be the TV room or our sleeping quarters, we must stand up until they leave or until they tell us to sit down if that's what we were doing at the time. This is annoying because they're always popping up on us and so we're constantly bouncing up and down.

There's a no talking rule. We're not allowed to talk to each other. If we're caught talking to one another, we can get written up, if the officer chooses to do so.

I can't become a working resident until after I successfully complete a six-week orientation phase, during which time residents must wear the same uniform as the general population inmates at Metro State Prison. The orientation stage entails attending workshops and whenever we're not in class, we must spend all day cleaning the whole facility, sometimes with a toothbrush, even though there's nothing left to clean.

When I finally complete that torturous, six-week orientation, I'm now allowed to go on interviews. I end up obtaining a full-time, second-shift job in a Sear's warehouse in Stone Mountain, and it requires me to stand on my feet all night long shuffling clothes.

Standing up working doesn't resonate with me. No can do! Especially after riding the public bus for over an hour to get to the job site. The motion of the bus makes me sick and by the time I get to work, I'm dizzy. So, I spend most of my time throwing up in the restroom or sitting on the toilet to take a break from standing up too long before I pass out.

By the time I arrive back at the half-way center, well past midnight, I'm dizzy and nauseated once again from the long bus ride back. I can't lie down straightaway because I first must take a breathalyzer test and then I have to strip, squat, and cough before I can go to my room and sleep.

I can't take this dehumanizing treatment much longer, especially stripping so these folks can look up my butthole every day. I'm fed up. And so, one day I blurt out to the woman looking up my ass with a flashlight, "I don't have anything in it but dooky. I wanna go back to prison and finish my time there. I'm sick of this!"

February 2001

The director of the center has resigned or retired. If it wasn't for her, I'd have probably been gone a long time ago. She took a liking to me for some reason, but the woman next in line to replace her couldn't wait to get rid of me for her own personal reasons.

So, after roughly three months at the transitional center, I'm expelled for insubordination, so they claim. All I did was give one of the correctional officers a piece of my mind with one simple word: snitch. And then bam! I'm slapped with a disciplinary report and discharged.

The news that I must leave the facility is bittersweet. Bitter because I will no longer be half-way free, allowed to do such things as wear civilian clothes, eat whatever, visit my sister, and sneak to the Perimeter Mall (not allowed).

Sweet because there'll be no more booty inspections and motion sicknesses from the bus ride to work. Be careful about what you ask for, I'm learning, because, as 'they' say, it just might come true. And in my case, it usually does.

After I'm kicked out of the half-way house, an officer escorts me over to Metro State Prison. I spend a whole week in the hole in the segregation/isolation building (a prison inside the prison) for being a so-called bad girl at the half-way house. Truthfully, I wasn't bad. They may have wanted to get rid of me because some stupid inmate who didn't even know me told them I was plotting an escape.

Since there is no barbed wire fence, a few days prior, another inmate had escaped, and they weren't about to risk having me escape, too, making them look incapable of running this work release program.

After serving my week in prison jail, where I am locked in a small cell by myself for twenty-three hours a day—in my case, twenty-four hours a day because I declined to go outside for one hour per day—I'm transported back to Pulaski State Prison to finish the five remaining months of my time.

The employees at Metro Transitional Center claims to have shipped all of my jail belongings, accidentally, to Washington State Prison. My friend, Angie, was kind enough to pick up my civilian clothes and take them to her house because you can't bring street clothes to prison. So, when I arrive back to Pulaski State Prison, I have nothing—no headset and radio to listen to music, no shower slippers, no journal that I've been keeping to write down my experience as a jailbird, no nothing. I must start from scratch, and I regret going to the half-way house, especially since it's now too late for me to participate in the computer graphics' program. I'm told if I want to go to school here, I'll have to extend my time and stay longer than the five months I have left to serve because the program is roughly eight months.

Since I no longer qualify for school, I must go back to work as a free labor slave. My new work detail is horticulture. I work outside mowing lawns and plucking weeds. But I don't want to be a prisoner and a slave, too, so I deliberately jack up the grass when it's my turn to mow the lawn. I made that bad boy look crooked, and of course, they can't have their grass looking janky, so they stop letting me cut it just as I'd hoped. Now I either fake pluck weeds or sit on the sideline watching the other inmates work like Hebrew slaves.

With the help of my son, who puts money on my books weekly, and my friend, Angie, who has sent me a package and money, I am able to survive the remainder of my time in prison at Pulaski.

CHAPTER 35

July 31, 2001

"Murray, pack it up!" yells a correctional officer.

She doesn't have to tell me twice. As a matter of fact, she didn't have to tell me once. I've been packed and ready to go since yesterday when I was moved to my own cell in the isolation/segregation building—the place where defiant offenders are housed.

I haven't even slept because I'm too keyed up. I've spent the last two years waiting for this very moment.

Do they really think I'm going to allow packing to slow me down from getting out of this beast? I bang on my cell door. "Pop open my door! I'm ready already."

On the way to the check-out building—where a twenty-five-dollar check, release paper, bus ticket to Atlanta, cheesy pink two-piece outfit, and cheesy pink Payless shoes awaits me—I spot Yo-Yo standing in front of the medical facility.

"Bye, Yo-Yo," I call out. "I'm gonna miss you."

"Bye, Vanessa. Write me."

"Okay, I might."

"And don't go back to that fat man!"

We both laugh.

"Don't worry, I won't."

CLOSING

My mysterious son survived the bullets sprayed at him during the alleged drug-related incident that landed him in Harlem Hospital with a bullet lodged in his thigh that has yet to be removed. The shooter was never found, at least not by the cops. Many more predicaments followed, during and after my incarceration, but somehow my son's life has been miraculously spared. While some of his codefendants gained felony records, my son has yet to serve time in prison and has no felonies.

Is his life being preserved for a specific purpose, I sometimes ponder. Is that the reason I was unable to abort him? It seems as if he has gotten away with too many things that most wouldn't escape, that most didn't escape.

What is to become of my son remains to be seen. In the meantime, he's no longer participating in gang activities; he's now an independent, self-made author and a teacher of ancient scholarship. He's completely legit.

My daughter loves to do hair and so she chose to become a licensed beautician instead of an unwed baby momma.

***

After Jeannette was released from Metro State Prison, I wrote her a letter to the address she gave me, the janitor's address, but I never received a response. So, I assumed it never reached her because she wasn't living there. I later found out she'd been arrested again for violating her probation and a new charge was added.

***

As for Yo-Yo, I never wrote her. She was a genuinely sweet person, and I'm sure her life has changed for the better upon her release in 2005. I wish her all the best in her endeavors, and I hope we meet again someday.

***

About a week after I was kicked out of the half-way house, word got back to me that Sierra went AWOL. She was found and arrested a few days later at a crack house on Candler Road in Decatur, Georgia and taken back to prison.

***

Lucifer and my antagonist remained together until her transition in December of 2006. Her final exit from this plane was due to a blunt force head trauma injury caused when she purportedly fell. Unfortunately, prior to her passing, Lucifer had been arrested more than three times for battering and assaulting her. She was laid to rest early 2007. She was survived by her three children who went on to live with one of their family members, and Lucifer went on to find another prey. Allegedly. My condolences to her children.

***

As for me, I didn't wallow in self-pity over the dumb choices I'd made on my fool's journey. When I walked out of Pulaski State Prison on July 31, 2001, an officer drove me and another inmate to the nearest bus station in Hawkinsville, Georgia. Before boarding the bus, we found a grocery store nearby that cashed our $25 check—the only money I had.

When the Greyhound bus arrived in Atlanta, Georgia, my friend, Angie—who never judged me but supported me throughout the whole time I was locked up—was standing right there with open arms when I hopped off the bus. I wasn't expecting her. I wasn't expecting anyone to be there because I had not asked anyone to be there. But I was so happy to see her.

Before I arrived at my sister's place, where I planned to live, I stopped at Angie's house where she fed me a nice home cooked meal, and then she gave me my bag of clothes she'd picked up from the half-way house. I quickly changed out of that ugly pink outfit and then she drove me to my sister's place.

It took me a good two weeks to get used to being free, but by the end of August 2001, I was gainfully employed and six weeks later I was in my own apartment in the same building as my sister. By 2004, I became a homeowner for the first time and by 2007, while studying for my master's degree in creative writing, I purchased my second home and rented out my first one.

Home invasions in Georgia were at an all-time high. The home invaders were kicking down doors daily. They tried to kick mine down once, but my back door was too sturdy, so they were unsuccessful.

By 2011, I was getting no satisfaction living all alone in my three-bedroom ranch-style house drowning in debt, so I sold it to an investor in a short sale transaction, and my rental property went into foreclosure. Trying to maintain two properties at the same time had become a bit too much for my budget so, I ended up moving to a gentrified neighborhood in downtown Atlanta in an apartment practically down the street from Martin Luther King Junior's birth home, now a museum.

In 2012, I sublet my apartment and began living a nomadic lifestyle while trying to find myself and gain clarity of my new journey and of the new person I was becoming after my twin flame awakening. At one point on my new journey, my twin flame journey, that is, I drifted off to Las Vegas to begin a new life there, but six months later, Spirit had other plans and guided me back to my hometown where I plan to remain until 2024—if God doesn't have other plans before then.

In conclusion, I bear no one in this story any ill will. In fact, I sincerely wish everyone I've met on my fool's journey Godspeed, and I'm sorry to those I've harmed—consciously or subconsciously. Please forgive me and thank you for your contribution to my soul's evolution.

I especially want to thank Lucifer. He played his role exceptionally well. He was relentless at trying to ruin my life. Sometimes, I can't help but to wonder if I'd done something atrocious to Lucifer in another life and he was evening the score in this life.

Even when I first got out of prison in 2001, he spotted me near the Underground while I was waiting for my daughter to meet me down there. He stood across the street directly from me for nearly an hour. It was apparent he was waiting for a sign from me, anything that might suggest that he still had another chance to finish me off.

I completely ignored him and when my daughter arrived, he slowly walked away realizing the gig was over. And I will never get back on that merry-go-round with him even if hell freezes over—lesson learned; cycle completed.

Most of all, thank you to my twin flame for awakening things within me I had no idea even existed and then afterward blowing me off. When he pulled away, ignored me, and treated me as if I was trash and not a special gift to him from God, it forced me to pull within to gain clarity of the real purpose for our connection, and it was there—Hermit Mode—I found the answer: one of the quickest paths to activation of the Kundalini and ascension process is via the twin flame route. The lovey-dovey aspect of the twin flame journey is a byproduct of the primary mission, contrary to popular belief. So, fixation on this catalyst/twin flame and the romance part of the journey and not focusing on loving yourself and knowing thyself will guarantee one thing: a life without your twin flame.

Lastly, thank you to everyone who read this tome. I truly appreciate you for not judging me, and I hope to see you riding through my next book—Twin Flame Journey To Self-Love.

Read on for an exclusive sneak peek
(a snippet) of a page from the upcoming
sequel to *Before Truth Set Me Free*

TWIN FLAME JOURNEY TO SELF-LOVE

by Vanessa "Fluffy" Murray

August 25, 2012

"It's time!" I heard as my head rested upon my twin flame's chest while he held me tightly in his arms causing my Kundalini energy to rise. He'd never held me like that, even when we, for a split second, dated in our early twenties.

Something strange had clearly come over Twin Flame seconds after he'd slid the dark sunglasses—the kind he always wears to look kool—midway down his nose.

When our eyes met, it seemed as if he saw something in mine that triggered something in him causing him to lose his composure as he surged my way like a frickin' metal drawn to a magnet, yanking me toward him, then squeezing me for dear life like I was his long-lost puppy he'd been seeking since the days of old.

It's time for what, I wondered. The only thing I could come up with, based on what I was experiencing, was that I was about to embark on a special journey and Twin Flame was a crucial player on this voyage.

Who in the world could've known we were much more than acquaintances? Certainly not I, that's for sure, even though I'd always felt a bizarre connection to him but kept it on the downlow.

On that dreamlike day, I knew nothing about twin flames, let alone Kundalini. Ain't nobody never tell me I had a dormant divine energy inside of my body and that Twin Flame had the key to unlock it from its sleeping state.

In fact, the first time I heard someone say Kundalini out loud, I straightaway thought it sounded demonic, and I wanted no parts of such a spooky sounding word.

I heard a crackling, popping sound as the Kundalini energy travelled swiftly upward inside of my body. I felt like a pinball machine who had no control over what was happening, as the divine energy zigzagged like a snake or better yet, an electric pinball, hitting what many call chakras.

Do I really have freewill? Hmm, I pondered in that moment. I was in total astonishment, wondering what the heck was going on, as I fell into a trancelike state, oblivious to my homegirl Purple—who was standing off to the side watching us—and the other roaming herd of folks in the park.

As he continued to clutch me, it felt as if our souls were merging before a third Divine, Pure Love energy appeared—tadah!

www.ingramcontent.com/pod-product-compliance
Lightning Source LLC
Chambersburg PA
CBHW030903080526
44589CB00010B/125